Advance Praise for *Live Your Bliss*

"Few people on the planet are more clear, more aware, more conscious, or more wonderfully insightful than Terry Cole-Whittaker. Her wisdom and her gentle, joyful guidance changed my life — and they can change yours as well, right from the pages of this book. I can't imagine any teacher in the world whose writings I would more emphatically encourage you to read."

— Neale Donald Walsch, author of *Conversations with God*

"*Live Your Bliss* delivers profound truths in a very accessible manner. It's high time that more attention be focused on bliss, which Terry rightly describes as the intrinsic nature of every soul. Terry is a wise woman who has written the most important book of her life. Anyone who has experienced her energy and enthusiasm in person will want to read this book. Anyone who hasn't should read this book, and then make a point of seeing her live or listening to her recordings. *Live Your Bliss* is a must-add to your personal growth library."

— Steven Halpern, award-winning composer, recording artist, and pioneering sound healer

"Terry is a master of manifestation. She teaches us not only how to give, but also how to receive with the grace that allows others the honor of being able to give and receive and continue the cycle. She teaches us how to create and allow our creations to continue to create for us and for others in a way that no one else has seemed to be able to communicate so clearly, so purely, and so effectively. If there were just one book to pick up this year on manifesting your dreams, this is that book."

— Dr. Eric Pearl, author of the international bestseller *The Reconnection: Heal Others, Heal Yourself*

"In this wonderful book, Terry Cole-Whittaker offers a bountiful harvest of rich spiritual truth. She helps us to realize the profound significance of every thought we think, every mood we indulge in, and every sound we utter. Terry takes us on a powerful journey of the heart in which we come to understand the role each of us plays in creating the life — and the world — we long to live in, the one perfectly designed to help us live in happiness, fulfillment, and bliss."

— John E. Welshons, author of
One Soul, One Love, One Heart and *Awakening from Grief*

Live
Your Bliss

Also by Terry Cole-Whittaker

Dare to Be Great

How to Have More in a Have-Not World

What You Think of Me Is None of My Business

Live
Your Bliss

PRACTICES THAT PRODUCE
HAPPINESS AND PROSPERITY

TERRY COLE-WHITTAKER

New World Library
Novato, California

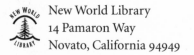 New World Library
14 Pamaron Way
Novato, California 94949

Text design by Tona Pearce Myers

Library of Congress Cataloging-in-Publication Data
Cole-Whittaker, Terry.
Live your bliss : practices that produce happiness and prosperity / Terry Cole-Whittaker.
      p.   cm.
Includes bibliographical references.
ISBN 978-1-57731-685-5 (pbk. : alk. paper)
1. Happiness—Religious aspects. 2. Happiness. 3. Success. 4. Conduct of life. I. Title.
BL65.H36C65 2009
204'.4—dc22   2009035584

First printing, October 2009
ISBN 978-1-57731-685-5
Printed in the United States on 30% postconsumer-waste recycled paper

New World Library is a proud member of the Green Press Initiative.

10 9 8 7 6 5 4 3 2 1

I dedicate this book to my spiritual teacher Haridas Sastriji Maharaja Babaji with deep gratitude for all that he has given me, beyond what I could ever repay.

I must also include my granddaughters, Austin Francis Wiesehan and Ahren Rose Wiesehan, in hopes that these two precious souls will learn the spiritual truths contained in this book and become eternally blissful and prosperous in every way.

Contents

From One Serious Pleasure Seeker to Another

*E*veryone wants to be happy, and this desire to obtain happiness is the motivation behind our every action even if our actions prove to bring us unhappiness instead. The problem is that unless we know how to be happy, we will become frustrated in our attempts and what was first a joy can turn sour and become a source of disappointment and heartache. I know, because this is what happened to me for most of my life. Things finally changed when I was given and started applying the wonderful knowledge that I share with you in this book.

We really can be happy all the time when we understand the art and science of being blissful and why it is essential. After all, it is the most natural way of living, and it also helps others toward becoming happy and prosperous. The world has been in a sad and mad state because we have been sad and mad — not the other way around. Most people believe that what is happening in their relationships, finances, career, and health *causes* their emotions. They live on a roller coaster of emotions and, over time, become jaded and cynical, thinking that there is no possibility for real and lasting love, prosperity, or pleasure. The knowledge that I want to share with you is that the outer world is a manifestation of our inner state of consciousness including our thoughts, desires, and feelings.

Especially now, we need to be as happy as we possibly can because something wonderful is coming our way, something that is dependent upon our doing our part. Doing "our part" means simply being ourselves. We are bliss personified. The happier we are, the better we feel and the more fortunate we become in every area of our lives. It is essential for each one of us to learn to access our divine, blissful nature, and then to express that nature through every decision and relationship as we move into this most auspicious time. Our happy state of mind and emotions will save the planet and bring forth the Golden Age. There is nothing to fear about the personal and global transitions that are taking place. The old is falling away as the new world is in the process of being born. We are the midwives, using our state of consciousness to aid this manifestation and transformation of the world.

Unknowingly, most of the people have been creating all the miserable conditions in the world simply by their fear and lack-based thoughts and negative emotions. They have no idea who they are as spiritual beings or the amazing creative and mystic powers they possess. All that is happening, including the corruption, war, starvation, terrorism, and other upheavals on our planet are simply a mirror reflection of our combined internal imbalance and unhappiness. I know this doesn't fit with what we have been taught to believe is true, but true it is.

Bliss is the intrinsic nature of every soul. Bliss is the key to personal and global transformation and transcendence into this new life and new world we have been praying for. We should not be hoping for or seeking out someone to come to save us. Knowledge has been given to each of us through spiritual teachings and sacred texts, but at the same time kept from us and controlled since the beginning by people in authority so that we would be in ignorance and thus easily controlled and manipulated into compliance. Our state of mind and consciousness are far more dangerous to earth and to ourselves than any chemicals and toxic waste. We must know that our thoughts and emotions are the very cause of what is happening and then we can, in a moment, change our future for the future is constantly in a state of flux and is being formed in this moment by our thoughts, emotions, and activities.

When people who do not have the answers to the most important questions of life are asked about these questions, they reply, "There are no answers, and life is a mystery." If you hear this from your spiritual teacher, I suggest you seek another teacher. Answers exist, and life is not a mystery, as is obvious to someone with spiritual vision. Everything is revealed to anyone with an open and inquiring mind who sincerely seeks and never gives up until she finds. Once we find, the seeking ends and our real life's work begins: realizing and actualizing who we really are — gods who possess all divine abilities and qualities. Then divine energy is able to flow through us and we are able to accomplish great works. The great opera singer Pavarotti must have known this. When asked how he was able to sing so beautifully, he said, "I just open my mouth and let 'it' sing through me."

When I realized and applied this knowledge, I started liberating myself from all the problems I had created. Imagine how good

I felt after my years of frustration while experiencing the ups and downs of being on that mental and emotional roller coaster. We are creatures of habit, and I was in the habit of trying to be what others wanted me to be instead of trusting and being myself. When someone would say, "Just be yourself," I didn't know what that meant. After years of pretending to be what I thought others wanted me to be, I had to find out who I really was. This required that I be willing to live without others' approval when necessary. Personal freedom requires us to follow our heart's desires and fulfill our divine, glorious destinies, even if others try to discourage or stop us. As Albert Einstein noted, "Great spirits have always encountered violent opposition from mediocre minds."

This knowledge has opened my mind to the limitless power possessed, not just by some, but also by everyone. Sometimes you may feel challenged by what you read here, but all I ask is that you expand your mind beyond what you have previously believed to be true. The value of spiritual knowledge is in the application, the experience. To this end, at the conclusion of each chapter I have added three practices — observation, contemplation, and suggested ways to incorporate the teachings into your life — as well as some prospering mantras. I like keeping a journal for my realizations. Perhaps this will prove valuable to you as well.

Something cosmically and spiritually wonderful is happening now. It is happening to us, through us, and as us. It is truly magnificent, and is something not to fear but to celebrate. Stephen Hawking has said, "The usual approach of science of constructing a mathematical model cannot answer the questions of why there should be a universe for the model to describe. Why does the universe go to all the bother of existing?" The answer is: for your ever-increasing bliss.

The following is my offering to you. This book gathers together what I have found in my search for supreme happiness —
happiness without the slightest bit of distress. My hope is that it
will help you find the same thing. May you be blessed with ever-
increasing love, bliss, and prosperity.

CHAPTER ONE

You Are Already Powerful

You and I are more powerful than we have been taught to believe. Each of us possesses creative powers that have mystical, even supernatural qualities and potential, and whatever happens in our personal lives, as well as globally, is directly related to how we use these amazing powers. As intelligent people, we seek to be happy and prosperous and to avoid pain and poverty. Doing so is possible when we know three things: who we are as spiritual beings, how life works, and our divine purpose and life's mission. Sacred knowledge offered to us in the revelations of mystic masters of ancient times, as well as our own realizations, are the keys that open the doors to the great secrets and treasure house of divine bliss and opulence. All forms of wealth are waiting for us in the form of knowledge that we can apply to get the results we desire.

Who Are We?

"Be ye as gods," we are told in the Holy Bible. It also states that we are made in the image and likeness of God, so we must be godlike in nature, possessing godlike qualities and powers. We are souls: not bodies or minds, but pure spirit. The Sanskrit phrase *Sat chit ananda* tells us that the nature of each soul is eternity, consciousness, and bliss. Whatever God is, we are too to some degree. Obviously we are not the Supreme Creator, but creators we are. Just as a wave is part of the ocean, but not the whole ocean, we are part of God, possessing godly qualities and powers, but are not the Absolute Controller. We already have the ability to be, do, and have whatever we desire, including happiness, peace of mind, and the intelligence to solve all personal and global problems. How do we solve them and find the happiness, love, and peace of mind we seek? There are three steps in solving any problem or attaining what we want: find out how something works naturally; stop doing what does not work; start doing what does work.

The universe and everything in it was, and is being, created perfectly. When we know how something works, we can work it as it was designed to work, and this includes life on earth. You and I are perfect, and nothing is wrong with anyone. But we must recognize who we are as spiritual beings, how we function naturally in our optimal condition as godlike souls, and how to use our supernatural powers. Once we know these things, we can attain our hearts' desires and fulfill our highest potential for supreme happiness, the goal and purpose of life.

But when we misuse our godlike and creative powers of manifestation, we create wars, poverty, sickness, unhappiness, and all personal and global troubles. In this respect, our powers are like electricity, which can light our homes and cook our food or, when used incorrectly, can cause a destructive fire. Many blame God for their problems, but each of us has free will. Free will puts the ball in our court: we decide how to use our powers of creativity.

This means, whether we use our powers for good or ill, the choice is ours.

Think of your soul power as having one "vote." Because all souls are equal and have the exact same amount of supernatural powers, spiritual abilities, and other qualities, all votes have the same power. You give your one vote to what you choose to believe and focus your attention on, and this gives that thought the power to manifest by taking on a physical form or a condition that is the equivalent of the thought. For example, dwelling on a fear will cocreate it in your world. Dwelling on your fondest desire for a home or relationship will *cocreate* that. I use the word *cocreate* because we are creating with God's energy flowing through our essence.

No one has more power than anyone else, so each determines his or her destiny by how each uses this creative power of manifestation. This is why each person lives a unique life, and why, when we join our votes, our creative powers, with those of others, we determine even the global circumstances of our lives. But no matter what others do with their powers, we always have the freedom of choice, and we use this freedom to cocreate our personal lives.

Each of us possesses several creative tools, in the same way that an artist has tools with which to create her art. These creative tools are hearing, thinking, imagining, speaking, desiring, feeling, and behaving. We use these tools all the time, and unless we use them consciously and deliberately to produce our highest good, we use them to produce troubles. Everyone — and this means everyone — possesses and uses these same creative tools. No one has more or fewer than anyone else, regardless of who he is considered to be.

Thoughts are the foundation of all personal and global creations and manifestations. Thoughts are concepts, and each has a specific vibration, that is, a characteristic emanation. When we believe our thoughts, when we accept them as true, these thoughts act like magnets and draw to us their exact manifestation in our world. The world is constantly changing to reflect the thoughts of the people in it. For example, we create scarcity by believing in scarcity. Everything is made up of energy, and abundance always exists — except for the persons who believe in scarcity. Our thoughts either open us up to our infinite possibilities, or they close the door. We get what we accept, because what we accept we act on; we create a vibrational frequency that must, by the law of life, bring to us what corresponds to our thoughts.

We Must Control Our Minds

People who are unaware of their eternal, godlike nature suffer from the effects of their sad and abusive thoughts and the mean-spirited words and actions of others. People die of broken hearts because they dwell on sad thoughts, when happy thoughts are the sustenance of our lives. Souls live on thoughts in the same way that bodies live on nourishing food and drink. Joyful thoughts are pleasurable and inspiring. Divine, godly thoughts give us good feelings and spiritual vision and intelligence. Fear-based thoughts of lack produce lack, and spiritual thoughts of prosperity and opulence produce sufficiency and abundance. Thoughts are creative because, when we believe a thought, then we take on the emotional equivalent of the thought, feel it, and act on it. Every action has a reaction, for cause and effect is a basic law of life.

Hearing is our highest sense, because what we hear goes directly to the soul. The thoughts that we hear over and over will, unless we reject them, become the thoughts we believe are true, whether or not they really are true. When the mind, the subconscious, fills up with limiting, negative, fearful, and lack-based thoughts, we believe these thoughts are true and close our minds to anything that does not fit into our accepted reality or belief system. When we hear, for example, that life is hard, then life will be hard for those of us who believe this; conversely, life will be a joy and pleasure for those who believe that.

We are the bliss of life, for this is our divine nature, the nature of every soul. We are nourished and motivated by positive and loving thoughts and emotions, and this is why we seek to be happy, to be ourselves. Happy thoughts feed us at the core of our being and cleanse our hearts of past hurts and broken dreams. All negative emotions and fear-based thoughts are destructive, for they make us feel sad, bad, and powerless. Acting on these negative thoughts and emotions produces unwanted results. In a moment's time, simply by a change of mind, a person can switch from being happy to being unhappy — or vice versa. People destroy their lives by dwelling on fear-based negative thoughts and emotions, because these thoughts draw to them the very situations they fear. Whatever we desire, we must be vigilant and accept only the thoughts that will give us what we want, and reject the others, no matter who feeds them to us or what we have accepted and believed in the past.

The most powerful terrorist weapon ever invented is an out-of-control mind. Anyone who exploits our fears can control our lives. Conversely, our greatest friend is our controlled mind, which we use for our purposes. We have a mind and a body, but we are not a mind or body: we are a soul riding within the computer-like system of the mind and body. We can use these tools, these vehicles, in order to live our dreams and attain full Self-realization, the actualization of our godlike nature.

Believing that we are only a body or mind is the source of all our problems. Misidentifying ourselves as a body or mind — forgetting that we are a spiritual being — is the source of all suffering, because when we do this we perceive scarcity, lack, and competition. But when we know and acknowledge that we are, as spiritual beings, superior to the world, we identify with our divine, eternal nature. There is an unlimited, opulent supply of love, happiness, and intelligence always ready and available to each of us regardless of our sex, skin color, the age of our body, education, finances, past experiences, religion, or nationality. To access this treasure house of spiritual and material riches, all we need to do is use our godlike qualities and powers as they were designed to be used for ultimate good. We are the precious children of Mother/Father God, but many of us live in mental, emotional, and physical poverty and suffer from every kind of abuse. Yet God is not punishing us and depriving us of what we need or even desire: we are punishing ourselves because of what we believe and act on.

Thoughts are powerful, for they are the seeds of future circumstances, events, and things. We move through life as we move from one thought to the next. Thoughts are stored within the subconscious as beliefs. Unless we know that the mind is like a computer, and that it only knows what has been programmed in, we can only be, do, or have what our thoughts permit, even if the majority of those thoughts are not true spiritual thoughts, and are false, limiting, and misery-causing thoughts. Souls are thought-generators; we generate thoughts by means of our emotions, words, imagination, and actions. Ideally, what we want is access to the greatest and most pleasure-giving thoughts and possibilities for us now and always. Why not, if all is possible? This means that we need to know how to access thoughts that will give us what we want and eliminate what we do not want.

I call fear-based beliefs poverty thoughts, for they deprive us of our divine rights and pleasures as children of God and make us believe we are unable to change the conditions of our lives, when we are actually cocreating them and can manifest something else if we choose. Poverty thoughts and limiting beliefs have been passed down from generation to generation. The subconscious mind, in a computer-like way, records everything we have ever learned, experienced, or been told; it categorizes things according to whether we like or dislike them and whether they are good or bad for us, and it determines who and what we think we must have in order to be happy and prosperous. This information makes up our prejudices and forms our decision-making criteria. But this creates a big problem if we allow the information stored in the subconscious memory bank to make our decisions for us or control our feelings and actions. The mind is not supposed to control us, but we are to control the mind by learning how to use it and also learning to discern whether or not the information we are being fed from the mind is true or false. We must place the mind in a holding position, which I call the transcendental position, so that we are able to use the mind to receive higher, spiritual thoughts and information. It isn't just what we know; it's being able to discern between what we know that isn't true and what is true. Our fate is set with every decision we make.

In the same way that we can be hypnotized into believing something whether it's true or not, unless we are conscious of who we are, and are awake spiritually, we can be, and have been, dumbed down, repressed, and misled into believing that we are limited. Repetition can be used for or against us, because whatever we hear, see, read, or imagine, and especially what we say over and over, becomes established as true for us, even if it's false. All else that counters what we believe to be true becomes, for us, unreal, not possible, even a fantasy, and false. But remember, all thoughts are vibrations that attract to the thinker the circumstances that are equivalent to those thoughts. No matter what we are told or who says it, if we believe it, then through our mystic manifesting powers we, as the generators behind the thought, empower the thought to create itself in a material form or circumstance. This is true for each and every soul/person.

Great Souls

Not all people are controlled by what is contained in their sub-conscious minds or by the words and actions of others. Extraor-dinary people are ordinary people who do extraordinary things because they believe they can. Instead of giving their lives over to others and letting them tell them what they can and cannot be, do, or have, these exceptional persons seek out the secrets of life. Throughout history the most extraordinary people have been the ones who refused to be controlled or suppressed by the words, beliefs, or demands of others. Anyone who has ever been, is now, or ever will be is another person just like you and me, with all the same mystical and creative powers that we have. Extraordinary persons are ordinary persons who do extraordinary things. What sets extraordinary persons apart from the majority of people is that they take it upon themselves to accomplish their objectives instead of waiting for others to give them permission or to tell them that it is possible. They are willing to live without the approval of others who do not have faith in them or their work.

Other people can be the greatest obstacles in our being true to ourselves and living our bliss, but only if we allow this by giving them the power to control our lives. Believing that our happiness, financial status, enjoyment, and peace of mind depend on anyone other than God and ourselves is misdirected faith and trust.

Split Personality

Trying to be what others want us to be, instead of being true to ourselves, causes a split in our personality, and this is damaging to us. A house divided cannot stand, and in war "divide and conquer" has always been a successful weapon. What this means for us personally is that, when we are torn between following our heart (doing what we want) and following rules and regulations that we believe we must follow to avoid punishment, we usually shut down and do what we have been programmed to do. When this happens, the soul is conquered, because it abandons its shelter, God Within, the Higher Self that knows everything. Souls must express themselves, must be who they are in order to be happy and self-fulfilled. But when we believe it is wrong to be who we are and do what we want — as if there is something wrong with us, and we are not smart enough or able to do this — or if we fear that we will be punished, the soul restricts and constricts itself. This is painful — the most painful experience of not being and expressing our beautiful selves.

When we are split between trying to follow the demands and rules of others, and finding out who we are and doing what is right for us, we become confused. The result is that we feel bad about not being perfect, or about not being good enough to be what others want us to be. But all the while we are perfect souls, complete with all we need to live abundant, fulfilling, and satisfying lives. We did not come here to live someone else's idea about what we are to be, do, and obtain; this is our life to live as we choose. The thought that there is something wrong with us is a cause of great pain, for we want to be loved. We want to feel good.

Self-alienation is the root of our self-inflicted suffering, because with our thoughts and subsequent emotions we stop the flow of bliss that is our eternal nature. Many of us are not doing what is best for us, but are acting according to social pressures and the demands of others who do not have our best interests in mind. It is common for people to do what they do not want, because they are afraid of what others will do to them if they don't. There is no beginning to the suffering that comes from ignorance of our god-like self, how we function, and how life works. But there is an end that comes with the sacred knowledge that has withstood the test of time, and which originates beyond the material universe and in the realms of pure Spirit.

When a soul is liberated from the shroud of ignorance, which acts like a cloud covering the sun, all neurosis and psychosis, all abuse and impoverishment, disappears. Misconceptions — which result in fear and a belief in scarcity, violence, and limitation — create a filter through which we view life, and they distort our perception of reality. In the same way that the sun is shining above the clouds, we exist beyond our concepts. The fundamental metaphysical teachings of Eastern mysticism and the teachings of Jesus tell us that we are spiritual beings of limitless potential, and though we have bodies and minds, we are *not* these limited bodies or minds.

When we know who we are, we can take our rightful places as gods, who use the tools of life purposefully and beneficially, rather than being controlled by the computer-like mind and body or influenced by others who do not know who they are. No one in her right mind would allow her automobile to take her where it wants to go, so why should she allow the mind to control her life? We can learn to use the tools of life — that is, we can learn how life works — by studying basic principles, or laws of nature, described in the teachings of the sages and saints, and by listening to our inner guidance system.

How It Works

We live in two worlds at the same time, the spiritual and the material worlds. Though we are spiritual beings, each of us is engrossed in a material body in a material world that operates by material laws. As a result, while we must learn about who we are as spiritual beings, we must also learn how material energy, which is also called matter, works. We don't need to become scientists, but we do need to recognize that the Hermetic axioms, described below, give us practical information that we can use to avoid trouble and attain more of what we desire. Everything material must, by its nature, operate in a certain mechanical way, for the universe is an enormous machine. But we are not machines—we are the operators, the activators of material, physical forms. Spirit controls the universe machine through the mind in the same way that we control the body and mind but are not the body or mind.

What do I call material? Anything that we can perceive and experience with our physical senses, or with any mechanical device such as a microscope, is gross matter. Subtle matter includes the mind intelligence, and false ego, which we cannot see. Subtle matter surrounds the soul and creates gross matter — the physical body that corresponds to the frequency signature of the subtle body. In this way gross matter is born from subtle matter. The mind in Vedic wisdom is the overseer of the five physical senses: sight, taste, touch, smell, and hearing. The intelligence is a different tool in that it is supposed to be our link between us, as a soul, and the mind (the computer to carry out our wishes through our actions). We are supposed to direct the intelligence to guide the mind. But what is happening, until a person awakens to their true, divine nature, is that the mind is controlling the intelligence and us. The programmed computer is controlling the operators, us, when we are supposed to be controlling the intelligence and mind. Think of the body as a vehicle for exploring the material dimensions, and the senses as the information gathering and experiencing tools. As there are gross material realms, there are also subtle realms, etheric realms, and purely spiritual realms. Each realm has its own operating laws. Understanding how material energy works enables us to act in a way that is harmonious with the laws of nature operating on the earth dimension, instead of acting in a way that is disharmonious and detrimental to us. If we don't know how life works in the realm we are experiencing, we cannot navigate our way around successfully; instead we are liable to be tossed about like ships crashing on the rocks in the absence of navigational knowledge and expertise.

The material universe works by laws of nature that have certain characteristics that we can observe and work with in order to attain what we desire. These immutable laws of matter govern anything made of material energy, down to the smallest particle and wave. These laws of nature also influence our bodies and minds because these are made of earth, air, fire, water, and ether. However, material elements have no control over us because we are spiritual and not part of anything material. Only our bodies and minds are material and subject to the laws of nature. Mother Earth is a living being whose body is the earth. Our bodies are made from her elements.

By recognizing the characteristics of material energy as presented in the seven Hermetic axioms that I discuss below and refer to throughout the book, we have a set of reliable guidelines for making our choices. These axioms are the conclusions of Thoth, an Egyptian deity said to be the heart and tongue of Ra, the sun god. The Greeks claimed that their god Hermes was the same as Thoth, and they renamed the axioms when they adopted them. Having an overview of how material energy works means that life becomes much simpler and easier for us to enjoy because we are riding the horse in the direction it is going, to borrow a Zen aphorism.

The Hermetic axioms can be summed up as follows:

1. All is mind.
2. As above, so below.
3. Vibration: all is moving.
4. Polarity: opposites are identical in nature, but different in degree.
5. Everything flows in and out.
6. Cause and effect: for every effect there is a prior cause.
7. There is gender in everything.

What follows is a short explanation of how each of these axioms works in our lives. With this overview, we can understand the finite — the small — and the infinite, or great. By knowing how the basic principles of life work, we can deliberately and harmoniously work it. But when we don't understand how it works, then no matter how hard we try, life is a frustrating and, eventually, miserable experience. Remember that, in order to go with the flow, we need to know how the flow works.

ALL IS MIND. The first axiom explains that everything is created and controlled by mind. "Mind" includes intelligence. We are consciousness, the Divine Spirit that is expressing — through our minds and bodies — our dreams, dramas, and desires on the stage of Mother Earth. Some people's minds and bodies are expressing their nightmares, but this is not necessary. Everything material is considered a creation, and we are cocreators who are creating in the same way that God, the Supreme Creator, is manifesting his/her thoughts and desires.

"All is mind" means that there is a superior intelligence behind the universe that creates and maintains it in the same way, that there is an artist behind the art work. The artwork does not create itself. Torsion physics describes the influence of consciousness on the creation and activities of matter. Until just recently, the influence of consciousness was ignored by scientists, but recognized by the students of metaphysics. We live in a sea of consciousness — the power of thought and intention influences what is happening in our personal lives as well as globally. Thought remains just thought unless it is powered by intention, the mood, motive, and desire of the thinker. There is a collective mind, which we can call universal mind. It works like a computer that holds all that has ever been known, created, or experienced in the material universe, including what every person knows, desires, and has experienced.

Our thoughts can affect others, just as their thoughts *can* affect us. I say *can* because we are able to shield ourselves from negative thoughts, and can access divine and universal knowledge at will, if we know how. We are capable of tapping into both the Divine Mind and the collective, universal mind. When I wrote my first book, *What You Think of Me Is None of My Business*, I had no idea how to write a book. But because others had written books, and because God, who knows everything, obviously knows how to write a book, I knew I could receive knowledge and help in writing my book.

"All is consciousness" is a more accurate statement than "all is mind," for a mind must be controlled by a person, a soul. Souls are made of eternity, consciousness, and bliss. "Consciousness" includes mind and knowledge but is not limited to these alone, for consciousness is a quality of each and every soul, and so it is godlike in nature. It's challenging to try and communicate in words what is beyond words and description. By tuning our spiritual mind to the channel of Divine Mind, God, we can receive divine ideas, solutions, and inspiration for whatever we choose to create. To do this we need to know we can, and then meditate, ask, quietly listen, and sense what comes to us. In time we can become expert in receiving the guidance we request.

Whatever appears in our lives begins as a thought, a seed, and if it is not a divine thought, then it is a fear-based thought characterized by lack and limitation. The mind generates thoughts from the subconscious memory bank, from the thoughts floating around us. Or, if we are wise, we keep the mind peaceful so we can receive the divine flow of thoughts that inspire, enrich, and empower us.

AS ABOVE, SO BELOW. This axiom gives us the code for figuring out how everything works, both spiritually and materially. It teaches us about the unity of Spirit and matter. Although Spirit is invisible to our material eyes, and matter is visible to our material eyes, they are also one within the all-inclusiveness of God. *Achintya bheda bheda tattva* is a Vaisnava teaching that tells us we are, inconceivably, simultaneously one and different from God and each other. One with God means we are eternally part of God and also different in the sense that we are individual souls in relationship with God and others.

Once we learn basic principles and patterns of human behavior and how life was designed to work, we are better equipped to make decisions. Life is not complicated; it works by specific universal principles and rules. When I understand how my mind works, I also know how your mind works. By knowing myself, I also know you, for there is one pattern for the human model, although within this pattern there are some variations. We may differ in religion, sex, body shape, skin color, nationality, and DNA, but we are also the same because we are equal parts of the same God and possess the same divine qualities and supernatural powers. We can know about ourselves when we know about God; conversely, we can know more about God when we know more about our true selves as souls. Whatever our Source is, we are too.

Because we are one with God but not God, we are the parts and thus godlike. God is the macrocosm, the "as above," and we are the microcosm, the "so below." One is greater and the other is lesser by the measurement of quantity; both are the same in quality. God is the creator of the universe and we too are creators, cocreating in the same manner but on some comparatively minuscule level.

In one sense I am you and you are me, but in another we are also distinct and separate, sovereign souls/persons. While we are all equal parts of God and thus made of the same Spirit, we are also and will always be individuals. Same and different can and do exist simultaneously. Think of snowflakes each made of frozen water and yet each snowflake is also different.

Taking this axiom further, the spiritual universe is the macrocosm and the prototype of the material universe, which is the microcosm. The Vedas tell us that there are planets in the spiritual universe, and we know there are planets in the material universe. Planets made of material energy are hologram projections of their spiritual prototypes, which are the pattern. Although planets in the material universe and spiritual universe are one in the wholeness of all, they are also different. The time-space universal reality is constantly changing, whereas the spiritual universe is a constant. Remember that the earth is a school that is patterned after the spiritual world. We are being trained for the higher dimensions of reality just as high school is training for college and college is training for one's career. Life on earth is training for life beyond the earth and material realms. Besides being a school for higher consciousness, earth can also be transformed into the spiritual for each person who transforms her consciousness from fear- and lack-based to love-based. "As above, so below" gives us the formula for understanding how everything works in the material worlds and also about the spiritual worlds. By this same axiom, we are able to know about ourselves and our creative abilities and divine godlike qualities by understanding as much as we can about the qualities of God and how God creates.

By observing how a garden is created and grows, we can understand how our creative powers work. Thoughts are like seeds. First we contemplate an idea, a desire, and then, if we believe in it, it's as if we have planted a seed in the soil. By watering and tending the seed, we help it develop through stages into a plant bearing flowers. But if we do not tend the seed, it will die. Thought is subtle, but when a thought is planted in our heart with faith, and when we have no doubts, the thought will take root, become strong, and develop into a life experience or type of relationship, something we want to attain. For example, when you get the idea that you want to take a trip, you think about it and make plans. Unless you change your mind for some reason, you will take the trip. It may come about through serendipitous events that happen in some mystical way beyond your ability to make it happen.

Thoughts move us from one object or one experience to the next. In this way the subtle thought gives birth to the gross thought: a mother gives birth to a child, and a garden gives birth to fruits and flowers. All begins with a thought that becomes a desire and is accepted, just as the mother's egg in her womb accepts the sperm, and the soil in a garden accepts a seed. Souls are seeds of God evolving and developing through our life experiences and relationships within the garden of Mother Earth. Gardens go through cycles, as does Mother Earth and all material energy. Bodies are made of matter and go through cycles from birth to death. Living in the material world, as George Harrison sang, is our opportunity to develop, by our actions, into supreme human beings, because our actions are determined by what we believe. Mother Earth is a school, a training ground for evolving souls, god-seeds.

How do we evolve? First we need to know that there is a grand purpose for our being here, as well as for our being who we are. We are told in the Holy Bible that we are made in the image and likeness of God, so if God is love, then we too are love. "As above, so below" gives us the key to understand that, if our Source and the Supreme Creator God is bliss, we must be bliss. God is prosperity, the reservoir of all opulence and power, and so we too have this same quality of wealth, an abundance of creative energy and mystical powers. Knowing this, instead of seeking outside ourselves for what we desire, we understand that most of what we seek we already are or have, even though we may not be aware of it. Once we are aware of who and what we are, and that life works as simply as creating a beautiful garden by planting the seeds we want to blossom forth, we can consciously use this model and plant the thought-seeds we want to materialize. Healthy seeds produce healthy plants, and weed seeds bring forth weeds. Happy thoughts produce a happy life, and unhappy thoughts produce an unhappy life — the choice is always ours.

VIBRATION: ALL IS MOVING. This third axiom tells us what science tells us: that nothing material is solid or static, that everything is in a constant state of activity and change. Everything has a particular vibration that can be measured. Our consciousness produces a vibration that attracts its equivalent in the outer world of people, places, things, and events. People, by their attitudes, produce vibrations as waves and particles of feelings, energy, and attitudes. Each person and animal has a unique energetic signature. When we learn to trust our conscience, our inner feelings, instead of judging whether a certain person is someone we want to trust or be with, then we are able to know by his energetic signature what he is up to. Just because someone talks a certain way and smiles does not mean he is doing good; he may be acting. We must trust our feelings and not his words; we must consider the things he is *not* saying and which we are feeling. Trust your feelings for this is God Within directing you.

Some people are difficult to be around because their vibrations are very heavy and repressive; others are fun and inspiring to be around because their thoughts and words are more etheric, of a higher, more spiritual vibration. Some vibrations are harsh and destructive, as in the case of cruel words and cursing, so these vibrations are on the lower, denser end of the vibration spectrum. Heavenly, feel-good vibrations are stress-free, and when we're around them we feel lighter than a feather and without a care in the world. From this higher state of consciousness, we are able to tap into the divine flow of thoughts, inspirations, and ideas, but in the lower levels of vibration there is only confusion and fear.

When we allow someone to enter into our energy field who

has a lower, violent nature, then we can fall into an unhappy state as we become like that person. Higher-frequency vibrations of love are much more powerful than lower-frequency vibrations of hate. One clue to being happy is to maintain your loving and blissful attitude wherever you are, and never allow anyone to take you to a level of consciousness that is not in your best interest. Mind control is most important — that is, controlling our own minds. Instead of trying to control another's mind and actions so that you can be happy, control your own and be happy.

Unconditional love maintained under any and all circumstances dissolves hate and disarms people. Consciousness is contagious, and we can use this for our benefit. Whatever we desire, we can find a person who has already attained what we want to attain spiritually, relationshipwise, careerwise, and materially. With frequent association, we will take on that person's vibration, including her knowledge, character traits, feelings, and attitudes. We can even get results that are the same or similar to what she is getting. What is transferred — like data transferred from one computer to another — is one person's belief system, knowledge, and predominate attitude and character.

However, the transfer may entail more than we want. Usually it is a matter of one program's being loaded into another person's mind, which is not a good thing, unless we want to take on the consciousness of that other person. Remember that consciousness manifests itself through the creative process on the movie screen of life. This is why it is always a good idea to associate with the greatest, most loving, and enlightened people you can find and would like to emulate, and to avoid negative, fearful, and abusive persons. We rise and fall in life by our associations through this principle of vibration, the transference of consciousness.

Thoughts have a vibration, and negative, fear- and lack-based thoughts are heavy and depress the soul. Elevated, happy thoughts are light and inspiring. Low-frequency vibrations of hate and anger signify a state of intense fear. Fear is the most limiting and dangerous of all frequencies, because it causes us to freeze rather than go forward with our plans, because we anticipate the thing feared happening. This would be like acting as if your mate does not love you, even though your mate is with and loves you, or acting as if you have lost your job while you still have it.

This is why it is important for us to ferret out any subconscious beliefs and eliminate them by understanding that they are manufactured and are not eternal truths. Otherwise we will keep getting what we do not want, because we will draw it to us by this principle of vibration. Whatever we desire, we must match that situation, thing, or relationship with our behavior. For example, if we want to draw a certain job to us, we need to know how to do that job, be an expert, and have the attitude and character of someone that others would enjoy working with.

Listening to the advice of chronic criticizers, naysayers, pessimists, doomsayers, materialists, fearmongers, and gossipers — the fearful, envious, and angry — no matter who they are or how convincing, can have a negative effect if we believe them and take on their fear vibration, attracting the very thing we fear. When we agree with someone, an idea, or a plan, we are using our vote, our soul power, to set the manifestation process in motion: we bring that thought into form as a thing, circumstance, or activity. When two or more people agree, this alliance of the gods, this gathering of soul votes through the power of agreement, is powerful. The greater the number of people who agree with an idea or plan, the more soul power there is behind its manifestation. The vibrations of thoughts and emotions pervade every atom of the body and act as magnets, drawing to us their equivalents in people, things, physical conditions, and circumstances. We may need to learn a certain lesson, and so we will draw it to us in some mystical way beyond our full comprehension. We can witness the process in motion, and as soon as the lesson is learned, the relationship may disappear.

Vibrations define the spectrum of what we will attain out of all that is possible. The vibration of our consciousness acts like a selection device that singles out the exact experience that matches our consciousness. The mind and emotions are the repository and battery of all human magnetism. Vibration teaches us the law of nature: constant change and movement. When we change our consciousness and behavior, the world around us changes to match the new vibration.

POLARITY: OPPOSITES ARE IDENTICAL IN NATURE, BUT DIFFERENT IN DEGREE. This is the fourth Hermetic axiom. The principle of polarity, or Greek two-valued logic, states that opposites cannot exist together, for one is true and the other false. According to this concept, if man is considered good and valuable, then woman must be considered bad and lacking in value. Yet both are good and exist together in the wholeness of the universe, each needing the other to exist. All paradoxes are reconciled when we expand our awareness to encompass the whole, instead of viewing each thing or activity as separate and independent.

Opposites create balance. Using this as our map, we understand that the material and spiritual worlds seem to be opposite, as if Spirit and matter are opposite, but that they are actually the same and different; one is the pattern and the other the reproduction.

As there are trees here, there must be trees in the spiritual world. As there are living beings here, there must be living beings in the spiritual domain, and so on. The North and South poles are at opposite ends of the planet, but their characteristics are the same. Each pole is a necessary part of the workings of the whole planet — the two poles are two parts with one function. The bodies of the various species, including those of humans, are either male or female, seemingly opposites, but are the same in all other characteristics. Differences in body type and functions are resolved as necessary aspects of one activity of generating bodies for souls to occupy.

Giving and receiving are two sides of the same coin but appear to be different.Giving seems like losing and the opposite of receiving or getting, but understanding giving and receiving as two aspects of one process, we can give to receive, and receive in order to have more to give. The axiom explains the various distinctions within the whole, the One. All apparent opposites are both one and different—all are valid in the unique perspectives they offer us. This ends all argument as to whose religion is right and whose is wrong. When we understand that all is one and different, and that seemingly contradictory perspectives are both (or all) true, we can unite all religions, philosophies, and differences, seeing them as various perspectives of the One God, the Whole.

Each point of view is true at a given level of consciousness and according to a given programmed belief system and set of experiences. All thoughts are valid; they differ depending on a person's perspective and what part of the framework of All That Is Possible she focuses on. When we understand this, we can have harmony in our families, businesses, and global community. Because each person has free will, each can focus, and is focusing, on what she believes in and chooses to experience; this is her choice. But in order to experience the fullness of what is possible, we need to know who we are, how life works, and our relationship with the Divine Presence and Being. Everything, whatever it may be, is included within the One — the Source and totality of what is possible in the material universe and spiritually — God.

EVERYTHING FLOWS IN AND OUT. The fifth axiom describes the process by which tides flow. Whatever we give out must come back. *Circulation* is another name for this principle. Blood flows through the body according to this principle, and the water system on the planet follows the same principle. Loving relationships are created by reciprocation, by giving and receiving. The outflow produces an inflow, and an inflow produces an outflow. When the pendulum swings to one side, it must swing to the other side. Business works in this way, as does money, and when one is stopped, the other stops. When we receive, we have something to give, and when we give, more comes in. Giving and receiving are two aspects of the same principle working together in one unified activity. This principle teaches us that what we give out comes back, and that how we treat others is the way we will be treated. From this principle comes the Golden Rule, the way to have beautiful relationships, success in business, and knowledge about how to develop our godlike nature of kindness, prosperity, and bliss.

CAUSE AND EFFECT: FOR EVERY EFFECT THERE IS A PRIOR CAUSE. The sixth axiom explains the basic law of the material universe — the law of karma. God is the original cause, the Creator, and we are secondary causes, creators through our thoughts and actions. For every reaction there is a prior action. Chance is another name for this law when it is working but unrecognized. As God creates in the material worlds, so do we. Cause and effect teaches us that every action produces an equal and opposite reaction. "Equal" means that the same thing we give out — for example, love or hate — will come back to us from the opposite direction, from another person to us. A flow that goes out in one direction will come back to us from that opposite direction, from another person. This does not mean that if we give love, hate will come back, although someone we are kind to may be unkind to us. When this happens, we have the opportunity to love in order to help heal another (but we must not take on their negative energy).

For this reason we would be wise to give out only what we want to get back. This is why the Golden Rule is taught in every religion as the best way to have a love-filled and happy life. Treating others as we want to be treated is the way to actualize our divine nature and raise our spiritual vibration, as well as to attract other loving and generous people. The effects we experience are reflections, similar to a mirror's reflections of our face and body. The effects reflect to us what is contained within our consciousness, including our beliefs, showing us what we really feel and believe. We can then make more conscious choices according to what we want to bring into our life or get rid of.

THERE IS GENDER IN EVERYTHING. Male and female genders exist in all species of living entities, including plants. Even language recognizes feminine and masculine words. Given the second axiom — as above, so below — we know that, since there is gender in species here, there is gender in the spiritual world. As we have male and female human forms, God has both male and female spiritual forms and attributes: God is our prototype. This is why I refer to Mother/Father God, for God is both one and two, male and female. Eastern mysticism teaches us that all living entities are female in nature; they are lovers of God. The feminine nature I refer to is a mood, not necessarily a body type, a mood of love and devotion, like that of a lover for her beloved. Because all souls are part of Mother/Father God, each of us has an eternal relationship of loving reciprocation. Science tells us that all human embryos are female at first; then some receive testosterone and develop male bodies.

There is one God with two aspects, male and female, lover and beloved. Using the axiom of circulation — giving and receiving — we know that this must be so in order for there to be the dance of divine love, the dance of creation.

Using the Map to Chart Our Course

There you have it, a brief breakdown of the seven basic principles guiding our lives while we exist in the material realm. Remember that we are superior to this material realm, and, because we are in it, we need to know how to navigate its challenging waters. They can be dangerous to the uninformed, but a pleasurable ride for the spiritually informed because of our free will, our ability to select and reject.

Jesus summed up an important lesson by saying, "Be in this world, but not of it." He also said, "Know the truth and the truth will set you free." The truth is: you are already powerful and always have been. Now go forth and use your creative, mystical powers as you choose. Be true to yourself, for this is all you have. A person who is not aware of the principles of life and his own supernatural powers of manifestation lives in constant anxiety, but one who possesses sacred knowledge and uses his mind to receive inspiration, guidance, and creative ideas is peaceful and enthusiastic. A sacred book of India, the Bhagavad Gita (2.66) tells us, "One who is not in transcendental consciousness can have neither a controlled mind, nor steady intelligence, without which there is no possibility of peace, and how can there be any happiness without peace?"

In the next chapter we explore the topic of abundance. God is the source of our unlimited and opulent supply of whatever we desire or need. Just as God has created and is creating millions of universes, we too can learn how to manifest with or without cash simply by using our creative powers in a prospering way.

Happiness and Prosperity Practices

There are three happiness and prosperity practices for each of the first seven chapters, twenty-one in all. In each category, you'll find one or more practices to pick from. Choose the practices that feel best for you, and create your own as well. Be honest with yourself about what you have believed, what you feel, and what you desire. Write your realizations in your journal, along with the main points from each chapter, so that you can remember and apply the teachings. We are creatures of habit, and habits are created by repetition. For this reason, use the tool of repetition to train yourself, your mind, and your behavior to give you the results you desire.

A. Observe what you think, feel, say, imagine, hear, desire, or do. Observe how you think of yourself and other people. Observe where these thoughts come from and what they cause you to feel and do.

B. Contemplate whether or not you have given your power away to others because you think they are better able than you are to make your decisions. What has been the result of allowing others to tell you how to live and what to do? Use the following declarations: Today, I will think of myself as a child of God possessing all godlike qualities. Today, I will train myself to remember that I am not the material body or mind. Today, I will remember that I am a soul, a spiritual being made of eternity, consciousness, and bliss.

C. Act as if you are a certain way, and you will be (be the way you want to be by acting this way now). Before making a decision, pause and then choose to say or do that which brings you in harmony with your true, godlike nature.

Prospering Mantras

Say the mantra you choose 108 or more times a day as a way to control your mind and convince yourself of the truth of who you are and what is possible.

God is my constant, opulent source and supply.
My nature is eternity, consciousness, and bliss.
I am enough, and I always have enough.

CHAPTER TWO

Receive the Abundant Flow of Divine Bliss and Opulence

You may think that people are unhappy because of their circumstances and the fact that the world is full of trouble. But in fact, the world is full of trouble because the people, the gods, are not happy. Happy people are kind to and respectful of others, while unhappy people are abusive to both themselves and others, and, either way, this affects the world around them. How we feel reflects what we think and believe, which motivates us to act. In other words, our state of mind and emotions dictate our actions, and every action has a reaction.

We live in a cause-and-effect universe, a machine created and governed by the Divine Mind, the Supreme Intelligence. What happens in our personal world, as well as globally, happens because of what we are thinking and feeling and then willing to happen. This is why it is most important for us to allow our divine, blissful nature to express itself. Otherwise we are using our creative powers to express unhappiness and, as a result, create more unwanted results and activities. The key to having a heavenly life is to occupy that life first in your mind and your emotions, and then by your actions. Be there now, and you will be.

Decisions made from fear, anger, or poverty consciousness must, by the law of creation, produce manifestations of these thoughts and emotions in our relationships, finances, health, and environment. Decisions made from love result in positive benefits and a beautiful life lived in harmony with the Divine Mind. When we understand that the results of decisions and activities that occurred in the past are bearing fruit in the present, we can choose to think thoughts and perform activities now that will produce future good fortune, using the same universal creative process. But we must choose to do this. There is no such thing as getting something we have not already earned by means of our consciousness and endeavors. Whatever we desire is possible when we work with the creative laws of life.

The first step in receiving is to understand that there is always an abundance of whatever we desire, regardless of outer appearances. Scarcity exists only as a concept, for abundance is everywhere. No one can even count the stars in the sky when there is a clear view, but when the sky is full of pollution all we perceive is a few stars, if any. The stars exist, but our limited and obscured perception, based on what we have accepted as true, blocks our view. The garden we call our lives may appear barren, or it may be producing weeds and poisonous plants, but if we sow the desired seeds — the thoughts of what we wish to attain and experience — these will take root and grow. Similarly, when we want to grow a garden, we do not sit around and hate what we have grown before, or indulge in guilt and shame for what is now growing, or worry about what we should have planted earlier. Instead, we go out and prepare the soil, pull up the weeds, throw away the noxious ones, and set about planting the seeds of whatever we desire to harvest in the future — and we do have an eternal future.

The Law of Prosperity Circulation

Water flows and circulates (macrocosm) on the earth in the same process by which blood flows and circulates through the body (microcosm). Once this circulation stops either by the outflow or the inflow, there can be no life. If a person ties a rope around her arm and shuts off the circulatory flow of the blood, the arm will suffer. The water system of the planet works on the outflow and inflow process. A lake must have a source that flows water into it as well as a river or stream for the waters of the lake to outflow into. When there is the balance of inflow and outflow there is health, but if the inflow, the receiving, is stopped, in time the lake will be dry. On the other side, if the outflow is stopped there will be flooding or perhaps stagnation, for circulation and balance are signs of health. In the same way, when the partners in a relationship stop the flow — their loving reciprocation — the relationship has no vitality or joy. Circulation is the process of outflow and inflow. And circulation — giving and receiving (two sides of the same coin) — is a basic principle of prosperity. Money comes from the exchange of goods and services, and if we don't offer any, then how is money going to come to us as the return, the inflow? Giving appears to be the opposite of receiving, but one flows into the other: they are two parts of the same principle that operates as a circular flow.

There is a continual stream of ideas, inspiration, and superior intelligence, in addition to love and bliss, flowing from the Higher Power to and through us, seeking expression. The Higher Power is always giving and flowing like a river, offering to us an abundance of whatever we desire, and even more beyond what we may know is possible. In order to receive what is being given to us, we must believe it exists and be willing to receive and express it, let it flow out from us as what we offer to others in the form of our talents, services, love, and encouragement. To whatever degree we are open, we receive, and to whatever degree we are closed we experience poverty, unhappiness, and lack. Our negative talk about hard times does not affect the Source of prosperity and wealth and what exists, but it does affect our experience of how much or how little of the knowledge, money, and happiness we receive.

There are three steps in the process of tapping into the divine flow: (1) become aware of the abundance of what is available to you, (2) pray to receive what you desire, and (3) start the flow by giving of what you already have, no matter how little or seemingly inadequate. For example, you may be feeling drained of energy, and if so this is most likely because you have created this feeling by means of your thoughts and emotions. Do something; take a walk, work around the house or yard, or do a favor for someone. Then by some apparent miracle, your energy level will rise. Souls are never tired; it is the mind and physical senses that become exhausted from use, worry, fear, or lack of use.

When we become aware of this constant and eternal flow of ideas, creativity, solutions, inventions, money, vitality, and whatever else we need, we can call on this flow to give us what we need and want. Brilliant ideas that will lead us to create inventions; answers to our questions; ideas for books, movies, and businesses; and solutions to any problem: all are always available from the collective information of all human beings stored in what is called universal mind. Above and beyond universal mind, which includes the collective consciousness of humankind, we also have the resources of the Divine Mind available to us in the form of knowledge, visions, and experiences.

Asking, or prayer, the second step, is the way we receive, for we have free will and can choose. Not even God interferes with our free will. Prayer is about remembering our connection with our Source, the Higher Self, and asking for what we need and desire from the reservoir of all that exists and is possible. Answers may come in a flash of realization, or in the form of an idea mentioned by a friend, or from an article in a magazine, or perhaps in a dream. Asking your Higher Self for something is similar to asking a search engine on the Internet for what you want. The search begins, and then all that fits your request is offered.

The third step for receiving the divine flow is to activate the flow, which we do by giving, or outflow. Outflow produces inflow, and inflow produces outflow. By doing the thing we have been wanting to do, but have been waiting to do until we get more money, time, energy, love, and so on, we will, by the law of circulation, automatically cause more of what we desire to come to us. For example, use whatever amount of talent you have, and your talent will increase. But if you wait for your talent to increase before you use what you have, your talent cannot increase. Increase is caused by outflow.

Remember, do the thing, and the power is yours; don't do it, and you don't have the power. Act as if you possess great love, and you will soon possess it. Act as if you are confident, and your confidence will grow. All seeds are small, but they grow once they're activated (planted). When we focus on lack, giving all our reasons and justifications for not having prosperity, we are affirming lack, which prevents us from receiving what wants to come to us. The key to receiving is to go ahead and act. Do something that takes you in the direction of where you want to be, even if you don't believe it is possible for you to attain what you want. Your actions will activate the flow of possibilities; inaction will just keep you stuck in the doldrums. The following two allegories illustrate this idea.

Let Down Your Buckets

Sailors on a boat at sea found they had exhausted their water supply, and many of them became so dehydrated that all they could do was lie down on the deck and pray for water. That night, fog enveloped the boat. The next morning, before sunrise, one of the sailors heard a small, quiet voice within him saying over and over, "Let down your buckets." Finally, the man got up and, in the fog, dropped a bucket tied to a rope over the side and pulled it up, thinking it would surely be full of saltwater and undrinkable. To his great surprise and relief, the water he tasted was fresh and delicious. Other sailors, too, dropped buckets over the side, and all drank to their satisfaction. When the fog dissipated, they found that the boat had floated gently into the mouth of a large, deep, and slow-moving river.

We may believe we do not have enough and are drying up from lack of love, happiness, and wealth, and we affirm lack by means of our thoughts, words, and actions. The sailor had to ignore appearances and do what his inner voice told him to do, although it probably did not make sense to him, given his past experience. He did something: he took action. He let down his bucket into the reservoir of the waters of truth, and it was filled.

Although this is an allegory for attaining material things, it is also a lesson in seeking our nourishment from the reservoir of all, the Supersoul within. We have a part to play in the creative process. Our part is to act as if we are prosperous, as if we do have enough to begin the process of generating greater wealth. In order to receive the freshwater, the sailor had to lower the bucket, fill it up, raise it to the boat deck, and then drink it. There is God's part and ours. My second story makes this point succinctly.

The Boy in the Well

A boy from a small village fell into a well. Hearing his cries for help, a friend ran to the well and dropped the end of a rope over the side and down to the boy. "Grab hold of the rope, and I will pull you up," urged the friend. "Will you put my fingers around the rope?" asked the boy in the well.

Whatever we desire, there is a part we must play in getting it. God plays a part: he sends the neighbor close enough to hear the boy's cries, and this neighbor brings a rope. The boy must play a part too, by grabbing hold of the rope.

We might feel that all is hopeless, but this is never true unless we give up and do nothing. When we understand that there is a continual, riverlike flow of life-enhancing, creative energy, bliss, love, and knowledge always available to us regardless of our circumstances, we can receive it, as much of it as we are willing to receive.

But we must do our part by giving out the very thing we want to receive. For example, a woman who had purchased one of the workbooks I had written came to another of my seminars after a couple of years and showed me the workbook. Every page was used: she'd done every exercise and filled out every worksheet, but with all this, she said, she was still not prospering. I asked her about her work and what she was giving to others in the form of a service or product. Her reply was that she wasn't offering anything.

This is why, even though she knew what she was supposed to do, she wasn't receiving. Why would we want more if we are not using what we already have? We all have something to offer that can benefit others, but before they can receive it, we must let them know what we have. If we hold on to the thought "There is not enough," then no matter what we have, we will always think it is not enough.

We must act as if we are prosperous, as if we are talented, as if we are and have enough — because we are enough, and we do have enough, to start the abundant flow of divine opulence and bliss. All things start small, like the great cedar tree that starts as a tiny seed and, over time, grows tall and strong. In the beginning of my career as a motivational and inspirational teacher, I held back the best information I had, in case I ran out of things to offer to my students. Then I realized that I was cheating them by not giving them the best of what I had. I was hoarding because of my fear that I wouldn't have enough material to offer in the future. Since that time I have always given my best, what I call my "million dollar talk." And more information, more inspiration, has always come that far surpassed what I had given out. It's been said that, in relationships, we hold back 40 percent of our love and care while waiting for the right person. This means we cheat ourselves out of that 40 percent, because we are not allowing ourselves to experience the fullness of our love.

Recently, a friend who had been upset with me for not showing her the attention she felt I should have years ago came back into my life. I love her and was happy for her — for letting go of her resentment, since any negative emotion is destructive — and I was happy for myself, because I enjoy her company. She is a wonderful person. I believed she had become completely free of that old energy, but then found she wasn't. At first, I felt hurt and started shutting down my feelings of love. Right away, I remembered that what she does is her business and what I do is my business, and I like to feel good and experience as much love as I possibly can. I opened up my heart and allowed the flow of unconditional love to fill it and my mind again. This is how we do it: in the moment, we choose to either react to people and take on their vibration, or instead to act from the place of love. Sometimes, there isn't even a problem but we have misunderstood the other person.

Turn on the Flow

When you think of this unlimited and bountiful flow, think of it as water flowing from your kitchen tap, and yourself as the handle on the faucet. As handles, we are the ones who turn the flow of water on and off. In this same way, we turn on and off the opulent flow of divine energy, bliss, and creative ideas, depending on how we use our minds and emotions and then actions. Although we are the bliss of the universe — for bliss is our divine nature — we can shut off the flow of bliss so completely that we die of a broken heart or develop physical ailments by constricting the circulation of blood or allowing old hurts, grudges, and resentments to fester.

Whatever we don't use atrophies. For example, stop developing your brain power, and it will be more difficult to remember things and you won't even try to learn something new. In that case, how can the brain continue to develop? Stop singing, and you won't develop your singing voice, which will then only prove to you that you can't sing. Stop feeling love or joy, and you will believe you don't have any love or joy — even though you are made of love and joy.

There is a great reservoir of effulgent life force being piped to you and everyone else; some people are using it, while others, who wish they had it, do nothing to get it — they don't turn on the tap. If you have a project to start, and you don't start it now, you will never start it. Remember, the secret: we get more of what we want by using what we have. If you want love, then give your love to others. Your feelings of love will increase every time you use them. When we stop the flow of love from us to others, we suffer from the restriction and pain of our own negative emotions. This pain is never about others and what they are doing or not doing; it is only about us and how much or how little of the flow we are willing to experience. Stopping the flow of love is painful. We are love and bliss, and when we refuse to be who we are, we suffer from the pain of suppressing ourselves.

When we turn off the flow of happy thoughts and instead think unhappy thoughts and experience painful emotions, what happens? Without this flow, we lack the enthusiasm necessary to accomplish our objectives and experience the love we must have to thrive, and so we shrivel.

What Stops the Flow

Water must flow for a garden to grow. Love must flow for a person to grow and prosper. Pent-up anger, resentment, remorse, and hatred, among other things, stop the flow of life-giving love and happiness in the same way that a rope tied tightly around a person's arm will stop the flow of blood to the cells of that part of the body, causing damage. Just as blood must flow through the body and carry nutrients to the cells, love must circulate through our hearts, minds, and emotions and embrace the people in our lives, as well as our projects, in order for us to live abundantly. What can stop the flow of wealth, the flow of every good and wonderful thing and experience? The answer is: negative emotions and fear- and anger-based activities. These include envy, criticism, anger, resentment, hatred, depression, blame, grudges, guilt, and remorse. Understanding what's behind various negative emotions is important enough that each one deserves to be discussed separately. When you notice that you have fallen into a negative emotion, first ask yourself why you have stopped the flow of bliss and love and then ask yourself if it is worth it for you to indulge in these harsh and dangerous emotions. There is a way that we have things wired so that when a certain event happens, we automatically respond in a certain mechanical way. Understand the wiring and untangle the mess starting with the cause and then you will be free of it.

I was talking with my granddaughter about this and she was saying that some of her girlfriends are suffering terribly from lost relationships. She said, "They will just have to go through the process of suffering until it goes away." And I corrected her by saying, "No, this is what people do who are not aware of the source of their misery and why they are doing this to themselves." Then I explained that these young women did not need to feel bad at all if their boyfriends broke up with them, for this has nothing to do with their feelings or life. I know this sounds strange to people who live soap opera lives as if this is a natural part of life. These young women turned the responsibility for their happiness and unhappiness over to young men who also do not have a clue to who they are and how life works or even the higher purpose to life. I shared some of what I am writing in this book, and it was wonderful, for she understood what I was telling her. We have it wired that this is what is supposed to happen for me to be happy and successful, and the wiring is what triggers our misery, not

what happens. Once a person finds the cause of these entangle-
ments and eliminates these misery-causing scenarios from their
mental computer, they can be happy all the time and free of the
emotional dramas that plague most relationships. I know, I used
to be immersed in these soap opera dramas.

Envy

Envy is like an infectious disease that contaminates us, makes us
miserable, and motivates us to be cruel and even hateful. We are
pleasure seekers. We want to be happy, and this is natural for our
nature is happiness. Jealousy is very painful. I know, for I used to
be jealous and suffered for years from the fear that I would lose the
man I loved or my position in my career. When we view life and
others from the material platform instead of the transcendental
and spiritual one, we perceive lack, and this always provokes fear.
Thinking that whatever we desire is in scarce supply, and that we
could lose it to someone else, we make ourselves miserable instead
of being happy for the good fortune and joy of others.

Envy means not being able to tolerate the pleasure that someone else is feeling or his success, as if this should be ours and not
his. The nasty essence of envy is: I want what you have, I hate you,
and I want you gone, even dead. More than likely you know what
I mean, as our minds work in the same way. Envy is the height of
mental and emotional poverty. Envious people are dangerous, and
it is best to avoid them if possible, for they are apt to try and sab-
otage our good fortune and us, as if our troubles will prosper
them. The way out of this envy muck is to notice when it raises its
ugly head and know it for what it is, a lie based on our programming. Rise above it and practice being genuinely happy for others
while also affirming your own prosperity. There is an abundance

of love and whatever we desire and need, so go forth and create it for yourself if you really want it. Being happy for others is a rarity, and the mark of a high level, advanced soul.

Criticism

Criticism is the constant search for flaws in another's character in order to prove that we are better. It is a symptom of envy, a way to diminish the other person to make you feel better as if there is something wrong with you because of what the other person is doing or has. When teachers, bosses, and parents give instructions with love, this is not the same as criticism. Such instructions given in love for our benefit are to be sought after so we can learn. The mood and intention behind a person's words and actions determine their nature. But criticism designed to make someone else appear bad in order for us to appear good is never beneficial. It's an act that will backfire on the critic because it is mean-spirited and hateful. It is our nature as a god to be sweet, kind, compassionate, and dedicated to helping others to be happy and prosperous.

Anger

Anger can arise the moment a person does not get what he wants or others do not behave as he wants them to. Anger is all about control in order to prevent the angry person from being hurt. Angry people are blamers: they feel that nothing is their responsibility, that everything is always someone else's fault. They fear being punished or hurt, so they remain on guard and ready to strike in order to protect themselves — or rather, to protect their false egos. The moment we decide that someone has threatened to destroy our false ego, our fabricated identity, we freeze. Then we suffer the pangs of our fear of death, the death of the false ego.

The basis of the false ego is the misidentification of the self as the temporary material body, mind, and senses, when we exist eternally as a spiritual body, mind, and senses. We must have an ego, an identity, and we do: we are godlike souls made of eternity, consciousness, and bliss, who are the devoted lovers of God. But when we lack knowledge of our true identity, we create another identity, a false ego. And this false ego is what feels attacked, for the soul cannot be hurt. The soul/person that we are is pure ecstatic bliss. When we feel our so-called ego identity being challenged, the false ego rises to protect itself, only because it is false, an illusion. When you feel challenged, when your feelings are hurt, when you are insulted, or you become angry, pause before reacting, breathe deeply a few times, and center yourself in your heart. Now decide how you want to act, what you want to do that aligns with your true, divine self, the true god or goddess that you are.

Anger amounts to shooting yourself in the foot in order to get someone to do what you want so you can be happy. Be happy and stop torturing yourself. You are a god, so be godlike. Once we find out what the nature of a god is, and what a god does, and what is possible for a god to experience and how, life becomes simple. Part of this process is to love others as God does. The axiom "as above, so below," teaches us that, as God loves, we are to love as well: this is our function, and what could be more wonderful than this?

Anger is an expression of violence, the desire to hurt another, but we hurt only ourselves by stopping the opulent flow of divine bliss in order to be angry and perhaps try to hurt another person. That's fine if you like being angry, for you are a god and can do anything you want. However, whatever you and I do in the material world produces a result; every action has an equal and opposite reaction. What I do to others will be done to me, and above this truth is a higher one: we desire to be kind and loving and to help others give up their suffering and poverty so they can be happy and prosperous.

When we seek to control others by emotional blackmail, by threats of pain, by anger or any other negative emotion, or by cruel words and any other sort of abuse, there can be no happiness, only fear and heart trouble. Next time you happen to feel anger, dissect it and find out the cause. Figure out what you are not getting and what you are using your anger for. Remember to pause before reacting, breathe deeply, and respond with kindness as best you can.

By making others responsible for our happiness or unhappiness, we remain on guard and in a state of anxiety, ready to punish the people who step out of line. In this way, we hurt ourselves. We are the guilty party: we steal our own happiness by stopping its flow because of others' actions. Anger is a powerful force because it is a destructive vibration, whereas kindness gives off a constructive vibration, a feeling and awareness of trust and safety. Anger in a home repels the Goddess of Fortune. In the Vedic culture, she is called Laxmi (she has various names in different cultures). She likes to visit a home where there is harmony, kindness, and devotion, where the inhabitants recognize human sacredness and the sacredness of all life.

Resentment

Resentment comes from anger. Harboring feelings of resentment for past imagined or real injustices will, in time, erupt in bursts of anger like a volcano or manifest in disease. Search through your mind and root out any resentments, no matter how small, and then hold them up to the light of truth. You may resent what someone else did or did not do concerning you or someone else. And yet, more than likely, you have done the same to others, if not in this lifetime, then in a previous one: what comes back to us must be what we sent out. When the results of an act come back to you, this is the end of that karmic cycle; the seed has produced its fruit. Be glad you are finished with it, and do not set up another cycle by means of hateful words and actions designed to let you get even by hurting the other person or persons. And if you feel you need to undertake legal action against someone, make sure you are free of resentment, or you will have already lost more than you could possibly gain: you will destroy yourself and your future with negative emotions. And in that case, ask yourself why you feel resentment. How do you think this legal action will give you the happiness you long for? Is it worth all the abuse you must take from your own resentful emotions and thoughts?

Depression

Depression can show up the moment we believe that our future is ruined. All depression comes from the belief that we do not have a future, that the future we planned is no longer possible. What happens to us externally does not control how we feel, but if we believe it does, then life becomes a roller coaster ride: we're up (happy) when everything is going our way, and we're down (miserable) when people are doing what they want and not what we want, or our plans do not work out as we wanted. This can happen when a lover or mate leaves us, we lose a job, we are ill, or something we were planning on did not happen. (It's wise to keep in mind this adage: If you want to make God laugh, then tell him your plans.)

When I was depressed, it was because I was afraid of what

would happen to me in the future; I had my worst-case scenario in mind. I thought if I died, I wouldn't feel so bad. Then I realized I couldn't die — no one dies; we live forever. At that moment of realization, I decided to find out how to be happy without the slightest bit of misery. Happiness is within the soul, not in the mind; hell is in the mind and not in the soul. An uncontrolled mind tortures us with the thoughts it generates, and a controlled, spiritualized mind is a source of constant pleasure and peace. Giving up depression is easy when you give up your expectations as to what needs to happen for you to be successful, prosperous, or happy in the future. Depression comes when we believe that our life is over just because what we were planning on happening does not happen. We have placed all our faith and hopes in someone or something, and this is foolish for we never know what is going to happen. Flexibility is most important, not rigidity. It's best to learn to put our faith in the Higher Power knowing that if what we planned did not turn out that there is something far better coming to us.

A person becomes depressed by counting on others to do certain things, which they then fail to do — or on certain events, which then fail to take place, or on anticipated money and glory, which doesn't arrive. The depressed person comes to believe that she can't possibly be happy ever again. If I start to allow my mind to terrify me, I quiet it and ask myself if it is wise to let my mind terrify me and, if so, what is the value in do so. Will the fear prevent the imagined problem or protect me from it? The answer, of course, is no, it will create the problem. The mind must be kept steady and balanced so we can use it to receive divine thoughts. Do what you want that gives you satisfaction, bliss, and good feelings, and do this with love for the benefit of others, and you will be happy. A depressed person is self-centered, resentful, and miserly instead of God-centered, forgiving, and giving.

Blame

Blame is the refusal to accept responsibility for our actions, for our feelings, and for whatever is happening in our life. We look for the guilty party, the one who did this to us, who upset us, who made us mad, who prevented our success, who disappointed us, who broke her promise, who ruined our life. We make this person (or group) the cause of our problems; we are the innocent bystander, the good soul who was taken advantage of. But it is certain that, if we were there, we had something to do with what happened.

The first name at the top of the list of those to blame is God's. "How could God do this to me?" we may ask. "After all, I pray and am a good person." The key to liberation and power is to understand that we have free will, and not even God interferes with our choices; not even God tells us what to think, feel, or want. By the basic law of life — cause and effect — whatever we set in motion by our conscious thoughts, feelings, desires, and actions will take form in the people, places, things, and circumstances surrounding us. And exactly what we get depends on whether those thoughts, feelings, desires, and actions are loving or angry and fear-based. God gives us what we ask for and earn by our own actions, but what this will be is up to us.

Once we recognize that something that has happened is a mirror that reflects back to us a lesson we need to learn, and stop blaming others, including ourselves, we can get the lesson and be grateful for it and to those who played their part. No one wants to be identified as the guilty one, for guilty people are punished, and no one wants to be punished. This is why a blamer quickly seeks someone else to lay the blame on, to avoid punishment. When you notice yourself blaming someone, meditate on why you are doing this and what you are trying to accomplish. If you are a sincere pleasure seeker, you will give up anything that causes misery to anyone.

Carrying a Grudge

Carrying a grudge causes you to feel miserable, so why bother? Someone may have stolen from or cheated you, but how is it meaningful to make getting even and hating this person the purpose of your life? Or do you do this because your life lacks meaning? Squandering our divine mystic powers on getting even, on paying others back for what they have done to us, may motivate us, but it can bring on physical illness and make us seem ugly. They hurt us, so we will hurt them. They ignored us, so we will ignore them. They criticized us, so we will criticize them, and so on. Some people would rather spend their lives getting even than succeeding in their careers and being happy. They may make maintaining a list of injustices their reason for existence, but in what lifetime will they wake up and smell the plumeria flowers and sing and dance in celebration of the Divine? It's time to party!

Guilt

Guilt comes along as the administrator of self-punishment. Guilt is our refusal to accept a positive outcome because, deep down, we feel we don't deserve it. But guilt stops the flow. This form of self-sabotage prevents us from using our talents, pursuing our dreams, and prospering, and it exists only in the mind. Stop punishing yourself, and go forth cheerfully and prosper. Stay away from people who like to blame you and make you feel bad. Most of us have something to be ashamed of. Once we realize the error of our ways, guilt and shame become counterproductive: they have a negative effect, not a positive one. God loves each of us beyond measure and is always our best friend and well-wisher regardless of what we did or did not do. Life goes on, we go on, for we are eternity. Since God is not punishing us, why should we? When we feel guilty about something, we must learn the lesson inherent in it and then apply it with love and gratitude for the realization. Once we've learned the lesson, the negative karma is over and we are free of it. There is no longer a reflection on the screen of life, for there is nothing in the subconscious to reflect concerning this lesson, you have passed the test through understanding the mistake in judgment and have made the correction in your thinking and behavior.

Remorse

Remorse is a heavy emotion, but it never changes the past; it only ruins the present, as do all negative emotions. The past changes only when we reevaluate past mistakes and see them instead as learning experiences. For example, instead of seeing a breakup as a heartbreak, we recognize that it was time to move on because there was something or someone far better for us. The breakup was a blessing in disguise.

Souls are feeling beings, and we feel either good or bad, in varying degrees. This tells the story right here — our lives have been about feeling good or feeling bad. Everyone wants to feel good and not bad, so why do people ever feel bad? When we expect people, things, and situations to make us happy, it means we have requirements that determine when and if we will be happy and feel good. When these conjured-up requirements are not met, then for some strange reason, we fall into a snake pit of negative emotions, build cases against people, want to get even with them, and pay them back for what they did to us, and so on.

All the time, we let ourselves feel bad, sad, angry, mad, resentful, depressed, disappointed, hopeless, and betrayed, and yet other people, situations, and things have nothing to do with how we feel and what we do. When someone gives you a disapproving eye, that person is in a disapproving mood and must suffer the consequences of her mood. But we don't need to react by feeling ashamed and bad — this is self-punishment. Why punish yourself because someone disapproves of you? If you want to make a change, then do it, but there's no need for you to suffer by feeling shame or self-hatred as your punishment. You do not need punishment to make you good; you are already good. All children of God are good, for God is good — pure, absolute goodness. Anyone who looks at you with a disapproving eye wants you to feel bad, but why? Loving people want us to feel good and enjoy good fortune. In fact, Self-realized people work and pray for our benefit, not for our demise and unhappiness.

If people only knew how fortunate they are: they get to be who they are, and they have the freedom to be sublimely happy for no reason at all. Because we witness so much violence and so many unhappy people around us and in movies and on TV, it appears as if this is natural, the way it is supposed to be. But it isn't. Violence and unhappiness are not what we exist for. Negative emotions never heal or help anyone; they actually make people sick, tired, and miserable. We are already blissful and prosperous — this is our eternal, spiritual nature.

It's really easy to be blissful. Bliss is what we are supposed to feel, and we do when we are being ourselves as lovers, not abusers, of others or ourselves. We are bliss. Instead of asking others to validate our worth by approving of us, so that we can be happy and feel good, we need to know that we are already loved beyond measure by our Source and eternal Beloved. We do not need anyone's approval or permission to be ourselves and do what we want. No one can stop you from being who you are and enjoying the bliss of yourself in your relationship with the Divine, for this is a sacred, even secret, inner love relationship. You can have as much happiness and wealth, both spiritual and material, as you want simply by keeping your mind and heart open and allowing the divine flow to be expressed through you. When we release all negative emotions, the flow of inspiration, creativity, and divine energy can be expressed through us. Negative emotions stop the flow, and then we suffer from the lack of love. We become full of love simply by feeling love flow through your heart out to others and to the world. The heart chakra is the most powerful generator that exists. Open the floodgates and allow as much love as you can to flow through the heart chakra and you are doing the greatest work in the world by increasing the higher vibrations. This is our work. Nice work!

Release the Flow

There is a reason why envy, hatred, anger, laziness, greed, and miserliness are considered deadly sins (mistakes): they torture the soul and kill the body. How do we get rid of stoppages and open the flow?

There are three steps in the cleansing process. First, notice why you are engaging in negative emotions that stop the flow of good feelings. What are you using negative words and emotions for? What is the motive behind them? Second, ask yourself if these negative emotions are worth having. What are they costing you? Third, decide whether you're ready to have abundance in every way by opening up the floodgates that have been stopping the opulent flow of divine energy. When we give up the notion that our happiness is given to us by anyone other than God, we can have an abundance of happiness regardless of how others treat us or what they say or do — we become self-satisfied, satisfied always from within. This doesn't mean that we love others close to us any less; we love them more, for hate and anger are gone. No longer do we judge that there is something wrong with them but realize that this is their life to live as they choose. Now we can enjoy people for who they are and stop imagining or wishing them to be some other way. The Bible tells us: "Judge not, and ye shall not be judged: condemn not, and ye shall not be condemned: forgive, and ye shall be forgiven"(Luke 6:37).

For-giving

I've hyphenated the word *forgiving* to emphasize that it means to start the flow of love again after we have stopped it in order to indulge in self-inflicted pain. While it may be true that the other person(s) was unkind or stole from us, our negative emotions do not change anything but only make us worse off. This other person may have said or done something once but we are torturing ourselves day and night thinking about it. When we stop the opulent flow of divine energy for whatever reason, it does not punish them, it is punishing us. Forgiving means to get rid of the obstruction that has been creating pain and difficulties in the same way that cholesterol clogs the veins and arteries and prevents the flow of blood to the heart. We exist for-giving, giving of talents, giving of encouragement, giving of appreciation, and giving of our wishes for the other person's unlimited good fortune. It is never about them, it is always about whether or not we are being true to ourselves or giving others the power to ruin our lives. The key is to always pick ourselves back up, shake off the dust we encountered in the event, and get going again. Envious people want to stop us from being happy and successful. Instead of moving on from the one act that they did to us, we continue to abuse ourselves perhaps even years after the person is gone.

Remember that life on earth is a school for the gods — for us. A school provides lessons. Our life tests take the form of decision-making opportunities. We pass or fail by how we allow the event or person to affect us and how we respond. Passing means we realize the lesson that either we have done this same thing to others or we ignored our conscience, God Within, and went against our intuition and guidance. Tests are failed when we feel like a victim, turn on the hate and self-pity switch, and seek to get revenge as our life's new purpose. Because the cause is within our consciousness and the lesson is always about unconditional love, when we fail the test it will come again and again until we realize that there is something we need to recognize and change within our consciousness.

I don't practice forgiving in the way that it is usually understood, because this implies that the other person did something to me that I didn't have anything to do with. I prefer to perceive what is happening as a reflection of something in my consciousness. This way I can make the necessary changes in my awareness and activities, so that the situation does not appear again. I am grateful to the person for helping me to make advancement. I know that if I do not understand the real reason why something has come to me, the same or similar situations will continue. The problem with forgiveness as it is usually understood is that the person who believes that she has been betrayed, cheated, or destroyed still blames the other person but out of the goodness of her heart she is forgiving them for their evil behavior.

We all know someone who is always the victim and always has his poor-me story of how others are taking advantage or cheating him. Until we seek out the cause that has magnetized this kind of situation to us, which is usually lack of discernment before getting involved with these kinds of people or making decisions that we knew were not right, the lesson is not learned. We tend to want to make others bad so that we can appear good in comparison. This involves laying blame on them for what has happened to us. We can do this but this is not the point, nor is the point making ourselves bad or wrong. We advance only by eliminating the cause of the problem in our consciousness and programming. Otherwise the same situations will continue to happen.

It's true that some people may cheat us, but we don't need to make the situation worse for us by worrying about it, or by dwelling on all the other injustices that have come our way. What kind of a life can you have when you are always thinking about yesterday and who did what to ruin your life? When we hold back the flow for any reason, we suffer the pain of restriction. Real forgiveness — forgiving others, God, and ourselves — means we open the flow of our creativity, our vitality, our enthusiasm and start to live abundantly again. Our river is full and bubbling over with blessings. When we no longer stop the flow, we no longer suffer from lack — we are enough and we always have enough.

We must view the outer world as the reflection of our inner

world. This means that whatever comes to us — whatever is manifested in others and events around us — is a gift from God, handed to us by karma. I used to be a fanatic, so naturally I attracted a fanatic in order to know what it's like to be influenced and manipulated by a fanatic. Fanatics are the scourges of the world. I got my lesson and gave up my fanatical ways. Real forgiveness is about releasing our feelings of love and enthusiasm with gratitude for having learned the lesson we needed to learn. We are grateful to the others who played their roles in the lesson we received, which perhaps could not have come in any other way. Get the lesson and move on with your life, which becomes better because you passed the test. The test is always to love others and trust our conscience to be our guide when making our decisions. We can even ask our inner guide what the lesson is if we don't know, and this information will come to us from what is called the still, small voice within.

Forgiveness is about letting someone off the hook for doing whatever he did, which automatically lets us off the hook. This illustrates the teaching that it is only when we forgive others that our mistakes are forgiven and we are released from our karmic debt. When something angers us, we must recognize that it was bound to happen, because its cause lies in our subconscious. If one particular person had not done the deed, then someone else would have had to fit into that position and do the same thing to fulfill our karma. If we stole from someone, we will be stolen from. There is always a perfect karmic fit.

More than likely, everyone has done something they regret and choose to avoid doing again. We could mourn our past forever, but this is not the point of our being here in these bodies. By focusing on past losses and mistakes instead of enjoying the blessings in this moment and each moment, we cheat ourselves out of the God-given gift of supreme pleasure that comes when we immerse ourselves in the freedom of self-expression that comes with love.

Forgiveness is the key to liberation. Admitting to our God within, our best friend, all our weaknesses, mistakes, debilitating habits, shame, and guilt left over from past activities, we can start to accept that we have been capable of doing harmful and cruel things to ourselves and others. Feeling remorse at this time is appropriate, for now we know what we did. When we ask for forgiveness and seek to make amends if possible, there is no need to continue feeling guilty or remorseful. Everyone makes mistakes, and everyone has secrets. The Supersoul knows more about us than we do and remembers everything we have ever done, and still continues to adore us and guide us in the same manner that we adore our babies and try to guide them in making excellent decisions. Once we recognize our error, we are liberated. The mistake is no longer a mark against us, but an essential lesson that, when applied, develops our divine human nature. Why not offer this same liberation to others? When we do, we too are set free to live in abundance.

We may not always be able to win others' forgiveness, because some people like to hold grudges and make others seem wrong and bad in order to make themselves appear better in comparison — they are good and the others bad. Their false ego identity is built around the concept that others are stopping them from expressing themselves, when it is they who are repressing themselves, and no one else. Competition is deeply imbedded in the subconscious, but this does not make it right or valuable. In fact it causes war, as if defeating others is the purpose of our existence and will give us the happiness we are seeking. It's all a matter of perception. Spiritual vision lets us see that all are winners — that we are equal in nature — and there is no need to create a loser to prove our superiority. We are already perfect and loved by God. Just feel good. No one is stopping you, no matter what happened or what others think and say about you. Once we know how to open up to the opulent flow of whatever we choose to receive and experience, it is time to expand beyond any self-imposed limitations and communicate the genius that we are here to express.

Happiness and Prosperity Practices

A.   Observe your motives for feeling sad, angry, or hurt. What are you trying to accomplish with these negative emotions? Observe how they have affected and are affecting you, your relationships, health, career, well-being, and finances. Observe the cause of any negative emotion you may feel, the reason why you are choosing to feel bad, and what you hope to achieve by this.

B.   Contemplate the thought that there is an unlimited reservoir of love, prosperity, and bliss available to you. Use the following declarations: Today, I will flow love to each person, animal, and plant, knowing I am the bliss of the world. Today, I will remember the happy and loving times of my life so that I can use these positive memories in order to increase these feelings. Today, I will release all the people that I have held in the net of resentment and feel grateful for the lessons they taught me. Today, I drop all self-abuse and give it up forever.

C. Act as if you are as you desire to be, and you will be: instead of reacting to what is happening, and allowing yourself to be controlled by the words, emotions, and actions of anyone else, take charge of your life and act and feel as you choose. Be an actor instead of a reactor. When you catch yourself indulging in criticism of others or in wishing them harm, stop yourself and remember who you are as a god on a mission of love.

Prospering Mantras

There is nothing for me to worry about ever again; all is well.
It is perfectly right for me to be blissful all the time.
I open my mind and heart to the abundance of love, happiness, and prosperity.
I forgive myself for all negative emotions.
I forgive others and feel gratitude for my prospering lessons.
This is my life to live as I choose.

CHAPTER THREE

Expand beyond Self-Imposed Limitations into the Realms of Greatness

*G*reatness is our destiny. Being great means being who we are. We are greater than we think or have been taught to believe we are. What is possible for us exists beyond the stars, for we are part of the Spirit and radiance that is the Source and creator of the stars.

A closed mind is the number one limitation of humankind. When a person is both unaware of and close-minded about what exists and what is possible for her or anyone else to attain, spiritually and materially, she limits herself beyond measure. No one can solve her own problems using the same consciousness that created them. A story about two frogs illustrates the value of open-mindedness.

Two frogs lived in a deep, dark well. They floated on pieces of wood and had the freedom to jump from rock to rock jutting out from the sides of the well. Their food consisted of bugs that came their way. One day when a person dropped a bucket tied to a rope down into the well to get some water, by an act of divine providence one of the frogs was scooped up in the bucket and taken from the well. Outside the well, when the person dumped the water into another container, the frog jumped out and into another world — of sunshine, color, flowers, animals, trees, waterways, people, and many delicious-looking bugs.

So excited was the frog that he immediately got into the next bucket to be let down into the water just to tell his friend and bring him to this wonderful and opulent place. However, when the frog described everything he had seen, his friend laughed at him and told him he was a fool, as this other place did not exist; it was a figment of his friend's overactive imagination. "All that exists is our well; there is nothing else besides this," said the well frog emphatically. Realizing that his friend would not come with him, the first frog said good-bye and left on the next bucket up to a new and glorious life, never looking back.

An Open Mind

An inquiring person willing to explore beyond what she knows or believes is able to tap into and discover the secrets of life and solve its mysteries. All mysteries and secrets are revealed to the person who seeks until she finds. This must be an independent search, not one based on a need for the approval of others in the family, community, religion, occupation, or nation.

Most people are imprisoned by their fear of what other people will think and do. This is the main reason why they do not explore what exists and is available to them outside their prejudices and the agreed-upon reality of the culture in which they live. But when we associate with the most loving, divinely intelligent, and seeking people we can find, this has the most wonderfully advantageous influence on us.

Four other primary influences also help determine what happens to us and what we create in our personal world, the planet, and beyond. These other four influences are our desires, our karma, God's will, and acts of nature. Understanding how to work with the five influences helps us to attain what we desire and thwart potentially troublesome situations. We can turn each situation into a blessing regardless of how it appears at first.

Influence #1. Our Desires

Desire is a quality of each soul. Desire is like the steering wheel on a vehicle. *Will* is another word for desire: it points to the goal, the objective. Through the supernatural power of the Divine, the way is made possible. We propose and God disposes by bringing about what we desire, often in mysterious and serendipitous ways impossible for us to arrange on our own. Sometimes the only action we need to take is to desire something, as long as we are clear about what we want, without any conflicting desire or belief. Philosopher James Allen has said, "Those who cherish a beautiful vision, a lofty ideal in their hearts, will one day realize it. . . . You will become as great as your dominant aspiration."

Desires are seeds of future harvests. The garden in your yard is the result of your choice of seeds and how you plant and care for them. "Don't judge each day by the harvest you reap but by the seeds you plant," the author Robert Louis Stevenson once wrote. Make the garden of your world as you desire. This is your creation, so make it as beautiful as you like by planting beautiful thoughts and desires. Dare to desire big things, so big that there is no way you can possibly achieve your goal by yourself, without the help of the Supreme Being.

We navigate the world by our desires. Because we have free

will, it is up to us to choose what we want to attain, where we will go, and what we want to be and have. Desire to attain what your heart wants, and not what others say you "should" want. We communicate with God through our desires. Pleasure-producing desires are those motivated purely by love, without rivalry or a wish to hurt others in any way.

There is nothing wrong with desire, because it is a creative ability possessed by every living entity. Most people have no idea about the manifesting power of their desires. Using desire in a divine way gives us maximum benefits; using desire indiscriminately runs us ragged, because the mind can conjure up unlimited, useless desires that are a waste of life and that can drain us of our resources.

When we make soul satisfaction our first priority and highest desire, then we find that all our other objectives are fulfilled as well. The Bible tells us: "But seek ye the kingdom of God, and his righteousness; and all these things shall be added unto you" (Matthew 6:33). This lesson teaches us to work on our soul development and our relationship with our God, and to do things that will give us the results we want, instead of doing what brings unwanted, negative results. Then everything — the house, vehicle, travel, resources, money, success, fame, or whatever else we want and need — comes along automatically.

There are several things you can do to maximize the manifesting power of desire:

A. Choose to manifest what you want to be, do, and have, and not what others want for you. We create confusion and cross-purposes when we try to be what others want instead of being true to ourselves. "To thine own self be true" is a recommendation that helps us to get in touch with our life's purpose, mission, and dreams. This life is our own to live as we choose. Knowing what we desire is a challenge if we have been told that we are not intelligent enough, strong enough, or capable enough to know. But you can trust yourself, your feelings, and your conscience. Develop the strength of your intuition, by which universal intelligence is known and revealed. This requires practice and trust.

B. Keep your most important desires secret. This prevents unwanted comments from others who may be rivalrous, or afraid of losing control over you, or limited in their knowledge of what is possible. Our minds are fragile in the sense that a discouraging word can cause us to give up and quit instead of pursuing our life's plan and purpose. When we tell envious people what we are planning to do, it gives them a chance to cultivate doubt in our minds. No one needs this. Keeping our heartfelt desires sacred and secret until they manifest allows a necessary buildup of divine power. Telling others what we intend to do, and bragging about it to impress them, dissipates the power, just as holes in a garden hose reduce the water available at the nozzle. Thinking about what we desire, and imagining it attained, increases our desire, which increases our motivation to act and ends our procrastination.

C. Focus your attention on what you want instead of what you do not want. Our attention is divine and gives life to whatever we focus on. When we give our attention to what we do not want, it thrives and increases, in the same way that watering the weeds makes them grow. Even if you are in an intolerable situation, shift your mind to what you want to attain. Let the river of love and bliss flow in you, and continue to work on your projects. You have a future, which is being created now. Because you can be happy regardless of where you are or what is happening, forget about hating anyone or any circumstance, as this only hurts you. You are free and always have been. Be where you want to be in your consciousness and activities. Then, when you have attained the proper vibration, you will be lifted out of the old situation and placed in the new one almost effortlessly. On the other hand, when we give anyone or any circumstance the power to make us happy or sad, to control our emotions, thoughts, and actions, that person or circumstance becomes our master, and we become stuck.

D. Accept that what you desire is attainable. Without such acceptance, no matter how hard we work to attain something, we just can't get it, because we are holding on to opposing concepts. You can't row a boat in two directions at once. One minute we say yes to what we desire, and the next moment we say no, because we don't believe it is possible for us to attain all that we desire. This keeps us stuck going nowhere except back and forth in the mind. Whatever our desire, we will have the power to manifest it when we decide that it's possible and perfectly right for us to manifest it. Our faith is demonstrated by our endeavors to manifest this desire, to do our part.

E. Dissolve your attachment to whether or not what you desire manifests. Do your best to bring it about, and at the same time let go and let God do God's part. We generate distress, hurt feelings, and anger when we are too attached to getting the results we want, as if our future happiness and pleasures will be ruined unless everything happens just as planned. Happiness is what makes the world go round — it's the motivating force behind our endeavors — but it doesn't depend on external circumstances. Nothing and no one outside of us can give us the happiness we crave. Always keep your mind at peace in the transcendental position, instead of allowing it to swing back and forth from success to failure, from "he loves me" to "he loves me not."

I park my mind at the third eye, the place between the eyebrows, so that my mind has somewhere to rest. From this spiritual position, I am able to receive divine thoughts and solutions, instead of regurgitated thoughts from the programmed computer of the subconscious. While some of what is stored in the subconscious is necessary, most of it has been programmed in, and it has no basis in eternal spiritual truths. Fear- and lack-based thoughts that dictate to us what is possible and what isn't, according to the programming, are not valuable but detrimental and grossly limiting. Everything always goes smoothly when we allow spiritual thoughts, words, and deeds to be expressed under any and all circumstances, rather than basing our decisions on concepts stored in our memory banks that will bring us trouble because of their lower vibration. You can look into your memory bank and remember a thought that you believed and set in motion by your actions, and that produced something you either wanted or did not want. Hindsight is always twenty-twenty, and with it we can see the cause-and-effect relationship between thought and action and then the reaction.

Influence #2. Our Karma

You determine what you do. When you recognize this, you realize that it is not, and never has been, a good excuse to say: "He (she, they) made me do it. What happened to me or in the world is not my responsibility; I am a victim." Our thoughts are powerful enough to create their own forms in this reality. The thoughts that we believe motivate us to act. Our destiny is set by the thoughts we believe and act on. Unless we free ourselves from the thought systems that condition us, we will continue to repeat our history like clockwork. Even a thought that isn't true will be accepted as true if repeated often enough over time.

The moment we act, the karmic wheel is set in motion and a reaction will appear — perhaps not immediately, but when the result is fully grown, which could take years or even lifetimes. Just as the seeds we sow in the garden in our yard take time to become plants and mature, so do the thought-seeds, which manifest when the conditions are right. "Everybody, soon or late, sits down to a banquet of consequences," wrote Robert Louis Stevenson.

Karma, cause and effect, reciprocity, and *action and reaction* are different terms expressing the same phenomena. Each of us has a cosmic karmic savings account in which all the seeds of our past actions, loving or hateful, are stored until they bear fruit. The Bible mentions this creative process: As you sow, so shall you reap. By this immutable law, pious works bring us good fortune, whereas impious works bring ill fortune. We are at the controls, and, through our desires and activities, we determine which of these will come our way.

We can desire whatever we choose. But to manifest our desires, we must have a cosmic bank account of good karma to draw on. This is evident when two people work the same amount of time and equally hard, but one prospers and the other barely gets by. The good news is that, once something unpleasant happens to us, the karmic reaction is completed, as long as we do not set another karmic chain of events in motion by reacting to what comes to us with any negative emotion followed by an action meant to hurt another person. Tolerance and forgiveness are most important, because they keep us from getting involved in all sorts of foolish unwanted karmic reactions. This is why Jesus taught us to turn the other cheek. Turning the other cheek does not mean offering ourselves up for continuing abuse, it just means being tolerant rather than getting all riled up because of what others say.

When we keep our minds peaceful, we don't need to react like an automatic knee jerk that happens when the doctor gently hits our knee to test our reflexes. We can act as we choose in order to attain the best immediate and long-range benefits. If we refuse to take responsibility for what comes back to us as our karma — our just desserts or a valuable lesson — this makes us impotent. The law of karma is impersonal and works only the way we consciously and deliberately choose to make it work. Why should we make our lives more difficult by getting our feelings hurt and reacting to the out-of-control minds of others?

The third Hermetic axiom — vibration — says that everything has a unique frequency signature that distinguishes one person, thing, or event from another. Souls cannot be measured, for we are purely spiritual and not of the material realm, but our thoughts, feelings, attitudes, and moods can be measured, for these are made of measurable subtle matter. It's our energy field that magnetizes or repels people and situations that resonate at the same frequency as ours. Whatever comes to us is drawn to us because the frequency signature of the person, thing, or situation matches in some mystical way our frequency signature.

Birds of a feather flock together because they recognize each other and are drawn to each other through what some call instinct, and what a theist knows to be the guidance of the Supersoul, Paramatma (the Sanskrit word for "God Within"). Because of this magnetic principle, we are able to consciously attract the kinds of people, things, and opportunities we desire, and to eliminate from our experience what we do not want by changing our emanating frequency. Think, feel, and act as if you are as you desire to be, and you will be. Be there now. This is how attraction, the law of karma, works and how we can work it favorably. The future is fluid, not set in stone, and we are forming the future in the present.

HOW BELIEFS INFLUENCE OUR ACTIONS AND REACTIONS

The mind is an altar on which we place and worship thoughts and images. Whatever gets placed on this altar gets our attention and motivates us to act in service to the thought or image. Unless we know the difference between what is true and what is false, we will place our fears on this altar, will believe and act on them, and in doing so, we will manifest the very situations we are afraid of.

We are constantly bombarded with thoughts, images, sounds, subliminal communications, and energy waves of every kind. The ones we accept, believe, and act on function as magnets, drawing to us their vibrational equivalent in people, events, things, and circumstances. Our own stores of information, whether accurate or not, flood our conscious minds with thoughts and concepts unless we control our minds by keeping them peaceful, so that we can use them to receive spiritual thoughts and guidance. By placing the tool of the mind in its right location, in the spiritual zone, it becomes our good friend.

Recognizing the falseness of any limiting and punitive subconscious programs in our mind frees us from their destructive influence. This is like removing rocks from a stream that have dammed up the water, so that it can flow abundantly and vitalize everything in its path. Living waters are truth, flowing from the source to us through our spiritual mind.

SOME SELF-PUNITIVE BELIEFS TO ELIMINATE

1. If I suffer enough, I will be rewarded.
2. If I have enough problems, then others will feel sorry for me, instead of criticizing me, and then they'll give me what I want.
3. If I hide myself and repress my talents, then no one can criticize or hurt me.
4. I should feel guilty and be punished for my mistakes, because I am evil and bad.
5. It is not fair to be happy and prosperous when others are unhappy and struggling.
6. If I stop feeling bad, guilty, and ashamed for something I have done, then I will do it again.
7. If I am miserable, then this will make others miserable for what they have done or failed to do concerning others or me.

Contemplate any self-punitive beliefs that you have and what these have cost you. By searching your subconscious mind in this way, you will empower yourself greatly when you stop holding on to self-punitive beliefs.

LIVE FROM YOUR HEART AND NOT YOUR MIND

Understand that, according to the impersonal law of cause and effect, if we are following our minds, instead of controlling our minds and following our hearts and consciences, then we are using our mystic powers to terrify ourselves and manifest our fears instead of our heartfelt desires. Even when something is false, if we believe it is true then it will take form. Turning away from the beauty of truth, we may accept the false as true and act on it, which will start the process of karma: action and reaction. Controlling the mind takes practice; most of us are habituated to reacting to others and to events instead of acting in a way that will bring forth both immediate good results and future benefits. Sometimes it is best to do nothing rather than to do something we will regret. Never allow anyone to force you into doing something that goes against your better judgment, because this will start the wheel of karma turning and will only result in trouble.

Influence #3. God's Will

All the ways of divine will are inscrutable to the human mind. Although we have godlike qualities in minute quantities, the powers that we possess don't have the scope of those that God possesses, so we cannot do what the Supreme Being is capable of. People seek their soul mates, but they already have a soul mate, the Supersoul, God Within, who always loves and adores us and never cheats or hurts us. This presence is pure love and ready to work with us in ways beyond our power to achieve independently. When our soul mate is God, then naturally it is easier for us to love others, for we are without fear of loss, abandonment, and rejection, which tend to exist in human relations and create anxiety. Without faith in a Higher Power guiding us and making our way safe and prosperous, we have only others to look to for our protection and maintenance, which rarely works out.

Supersoul is the Soul of every individual soul. As each individual ray of sunlight emanates from the same sun, we are individual rays of Spirit emanating from the same Source, which we call God. Every living entity has the same Supreme Soul regardless of body type, sex, nationality, or religion. This is why, when we seek guidance and assistance from the God presence within us, the right people and situations come to us and we receive information far beyond just our prior knowledge or experience. God knows everyone and everything and, in every situation, what is our highest good.

FAITH

Wherefore, if God so clothe the grass of the field,
which to-day is, and to-morrow is cast into the oven,
[shall he] not much more [clothe] you,
O ye of little faith. And he said unto them,
Why are ye so fearful? How is it that ye have no faith?

MATTHEW 6:30

Faith is each soul's manifesting power. This is why certain people work so hard to get us to believe in them and what they say. By using divine logic, we can discern whether others are telling the truth or not, and if what they are telling us is being used to manipulate us into doing something that will hurt or cheat us or really help us. Of course, in order to obtain our faith, our soul manifesting power, people who are up to no good will tell us that what they are proposing or selling is in our best interest.

One way that those up to no good get us to have faith in them, and in what they want to sell us or get us to do, is by creating a fictitious problem and dramatizing it to make it seem to be a real danger, one that frightens us. Then they present their solution, and we are so grateful that they have come to save us that we agree to buy or go along with what these people are proposing. Religious leaders of old did this to control people through fear, but this is never right and always wrong, for God is kind and gentle and the well-wisher of all, not the vicious, cruel-hearted God that some have created in their own minds in order to demand compliance from the faithful and simple hearted.

God's will for us is always for us to attain our highest good, including our happiness, good health, and prosperity, but this may not be the will of others. Because we are part of God, and God knows everyone and everything, God knows what will give us the greatest pleasure and good fortune and is always working to bring us to this state of total and eternal bliss, which comes when we unify in mind and heart with our Beloved. Our purpose and function are simply to love God and be loved by God, and then everything else falls into place effortlessly.

THY WILL BE DONE

When I pray and ask for what I desire, I always ask that God's will be done. While accepting and having faith that what I have asked for I will receive, I also am willing to receive what is better for me spiritually and materially than what I have asked for, because I know that the Supreme Being is enormously more powerful than I or all souls combined. A request like this keeps us open to receiving greater benefits and brings us into direct alignment with what is ultimately possible for us. God, who creates and maintains billions of universes without our help, can certainly help us far beyond what we can do for ourselves alone. When we make God our partner, all things are possible for us. We need to put our faith in who and what is the greatest, and not in someone else's opinion or even in our own, if that opinion limits us in any way spiritually or materially.

SELF-PUNISHMENT

God does not judge and punish us; we judge ourselves and administer our own punishment. Shame and guilt for our so-called past mistakes can cause us to be too embarrassed to face God, to come back home and receive all that God is offering us, which is beyond measure and incalculable by human standards. The fear-based and angry-God programming may be so strong in us that we may think it is better to hide from God, to ignore God, than to turn and face our Beloved, who wants only to love us and be loved in return. Loving reciprocation is the essence of every satisfying relationship. Why not have a reciprocal relationship with your eternal, loving soul mate, who really loves you unconditionally as you are?

The idea that God is angry and must be pacified by means of blood sacrifice and violence against others came from the teachings of Zoroaster, an ancient prophet and religious poet from Babylon. His teachings about an angry, vengeful, and cruel God found their way into Judaism, Islam, and Christianity, polluting the pure message about divine love and our holy nature. This cruel concept of God, and the idea that violence is God's plan for humanity, has driven, and is still driving, people to commit atrocities against others and justify genocide for the sake of money, power, sex, sensual pleasures, and domination. Any religion that teaches hatred of others, that says some are chosen and others are not, that says one body type is superior to another, or says that people must war against and destroy anyone who is not of their faith is false. It creates hell on earth instead of heaven.

God can do anything beyond the laws of the universe, for God created the universe and maintains it, and is not subject to human laws, rules, regulations, or values. Caitanya, an avatar and saint living in India in the fifteenth century, was a living example of how to love God with all your heart, soul, mind, and strength. Many historians of his time wrote about him and acclaimed him as the most ecstatically blissful person who had ever lived. Caitanya predicted a ten-thousand-year golden age. He prescribed a cure for troubles of the world, saying, "Sing the holy names of God with love and devotion, dance in ecstasy, feast, and be happy."

We, as God's children, really are supposed to be singing, dancing, and celebrating life in the kingdom of God that is all around us. It's all about perception. Perceive hell and you live in hell. Perceive heaven, and God everywhere, and you are in heaven. Yes, we have permission from on high to celebrate life instead of working like robotic, mind-controlled slaves and buying stuff we have been programmed to believe we must have in order to be happy, when we can just be happy and do what we want. All we need comes to us when we are engaged in doing our life's work as an offering to God and others for their pleasure.

Influence #4. Acts of Nature

Calling an act of nature an act of God is not entirely accurate, as there is a distinction between an act of nature and an act of God. Distinctions are important. Although God creates nature through his material energy, we also have some measure of influence on what happens to us through nature. Because we are surrounded by material nature, we need to know something about the various creatures and acts of nature that can affect us in the regions where we live or travel. For example, a person swimming in the ocean could be caught in a riptide. If he knows how to swim well and understands the characteristics of a riptide, he will escape, and it will be an adventure. On the other hand, if he is a weak swimmer and has no idea how to free himself from a riptide, he could lose his body. His being caught in the riptide is not an act of nature, although the water is an aspect of, and so a part of, nature.

A rainstorm is an act of nature, but whether or not this rain floods our home is determined by where our home is located — how close to a river — or in the case of modern-day flooding, the result of human intervention. Construction of shopping centers, industrial buildings, or housing projects on the ground that was a riverbed or on an area of land that had provided a natural absorption field for excessive water will cause flooding where this had never happened before. Believing that the rain that destroys someone's home is completely an act of God, as if God likes destroying people's homes and causing them difficulties, is not the proper way to view a loving and sweet God. It also implies that we have nothing to do with what happens in nature. This gives God a bad name and generates hatred for God.

Weather modification is common practice in the United States and perhaps among governments in other countries as well.

Scientists are hired to manipulate the laws of nature in certain ways, even as a weapon. We cannot blame God for all the atrocities caused by humans, for God gives us free will. God and the higher beings will help us if we ask, and we also must do our part.

Human intervention includes cutting down trees and not replanting. Later, when it rains, the topsoil, having no trees or roots to protect it, will flow into the rivers, clogging them and stripping the land of precious topsoil. The Aswan dam in Egypt has brought enormous troubles to the people near it and their way of life, even causing diseases and insect infestations of the sort that formerly were controlled by the natural flooding of the Nile. This dam was made to create electric power that could be sold to people with the promise of improving their lives and providing them with more prosperity, but this promise hasn't been fulfilled. The dam has done the opposite, as has everything that we humans have done that goes against the natural order and harmony of life on earth. Before the dam was built, there was always enough for everyone.

Nature works on the principle of circulation, which can be understood as balance. When nature is in balance, there is an abundance of food, clean air, and water, and life is good all around. This is explained by the fifth Hermetic axiom. When the pendulum swings to one side, it will swing to the other to keep the balance. The greater the swing in one direction, the greater the degree of swing to the opposite side. Everything is seeking balance to even out the score and come back to center and harmony.

When pollution is great, the cleansing must also be great in order to restore balance, health. One extreme creates another extreme in order to bring stability and balance. There really is no global warming created by humans; sun flares create it. When there is warming on our planet, there is a warming on all planets in this solar system. And when there is a lessening of sun flares, there is a cold period on earth and throughout the solar system. Nature works in cycles according to the laws of nature, which are created by God and managed by angels, nature spirits, demigods, and higher beings.

We may not know what Mother Earth or her creatures are going to do at any given moment, but it's important to know what to do in an emergency and how to work in harmony with nature. Ignorance is not bliss — it's asking for trouble. As strange as it may seem, given what we have been trained to believe about nature, God does not create destructive weather and earth changes to bring pain to the inhabitants. Calling global disasters "acts of God" is blasphemy, for many disasters are the result of human error. Earth is an amazing aerial mansion, a spacecraft, that I call a garden planet. Some scientists have found that the earth is larger than it was, and so she is understood to be a living being.

When human beings understand their position in nature as caretakers of Mother/Father God's creation, and they live in harmony with nature, nature is balanced and there is an abundance of rain, sunshine, and food for all the creatures in the garden and school yard. I believe that our consciousness influences every aspect of what is happening everywhere, for all is consciousness, including thoughts, emotions, and our actions. Every aspect of nature, including the insects, rodents, other animals, and plants, has a right to live and is necessary in the grand scheme of things, the evolution of souls. Every creature great and small has a right to live out its life in this world peacefully and prosperously, not just a few of us. Our mission, as human beings, as children of God, is to work for the welfare of all others, including all the animals and plants. The universe and everything in it is one whole unit that works by *symbiosis* (from the Greek *symbioun*, "to live together"), the term for the interdependence of different species, which are sometimes called *symbionts* — it is a cocreating partnership.

At my organic farm in Washington State, miracles happened when we used only natural ways to build the soil and grow the garden. Within two years, our main gardener, Reuben, regenerated barren soil, turning it into rich soil that produced an overabundance of food, flowers, and beauty. As our farm became more ecologically balanced, we saw more and more demonstrations of the presence of nature spirits, as well as mystical phenomena.

Indigenous cultures know about the symbiotic relationship between humans and Mother Earth and her creatures. These cultures appreciate each of the life-forms and pay homage to them with prayers, spiritual activities, respect, and care. Vedic, Celtic, Aboriginal, and Native American rituals and chants honoring the elements, directions, and devas are still part of these spiritual practices. Presently, devas are more commonly thought of as nature spirits. There seems to be a cooperative partnership between devas and human beings and ecological balance. This partnership was discovered in the produce of Findhorn in Scotland and of Perelandra in Washington, D.C. It seems that devas are the "architects" of nature, and their part is essential in the grand scheme of things. A deva is in charge of every element and process of nature on earth, even the soil and water. In Vedic teachings, devas are called demigods. They are the blueprint designers for all living things and control all necessary energies for growth and maintenance. They also deliver the rain that produces the grains and other foods.

We may not perceive these nature spirits or the celestial hierarchy with our material eyes and senses, but this does not mean they do not exist. No one can see the wind, but we can feel the presence of the wind as it blows across our skin, and we can see the shaking of the leaves on a tree. Likewise, we can experience the effects of nature spirits' presence.

The Vedic and Essene practices of offering clarified butter, grains, and dry cow dung into a small fire at dawn and sunset are believed to bring balance to the ecology. (The Essenes were one of the three sects of Judaism in the time of Jesus and still exist today.) We must learn to understand that life is a spiritual and mystical experience, not a science project in which all is diminished to the lowest common denominator of numbers. Consciousness is behind all phenomena — it's a dance of love between the male and female aspects of the One God being expressed through limitless numbers of beings.

Vaastu, a Vedic science, is similar to feng shui in that it takes the energy system of the planet into consideration. Both are methods of aligning one's home and other structures according to the energy lines of the earth because these affect the functions performed in each section of the home and property. Earth, people, microwaves and other machines, cell phones and other electronics, X-ray equipment, and all chemicals emanate vibrations that have an effect on the body and brain. For this reason, we should help to balance the energies in our homes, in our offices, and on our land to give ourselves the optimal conditions for peace, intelligence, and prosperity by eliminating dangerous vibrations and harmonizing the energy flows. The government of China knows this and is designing buildings according to the principles of feng shui. Remember that whatever we do to the earth and the elements we are also doing to our bodies and minds, and whatever we are doing to our bodies and minds, we are also doing to the earth and her inhabitants. All is part of the One, the whole system.

Influence #5. Other People

Associating with the most intelligent, loving, and spiritually enlightened people possible, either in person or via their books and teachings, is the best and fastest way for us to advance, whatever the goal. We rise and fall by our associations, because consciousness is contagious. When we associate with greatness, we become great. When we associate with the angry, envious, and degraded, we too can become angry, envious, and degraded if we allow it. When we are unaware of the influence that others can have on us, we are like sponges soaking up their emotions, beliefs, and words without discrimination. "Garbage in and garbage out" is a computer term that sums up this lesson. The moment we believe and then act on information we receive from any person, we become shaped by that information.

Sri Aurobindo, a Vedic saint and teacher who left this world in 1950, explained: "Every one of us burdens a horrible weight of external pressure and rules and laws. In every moment from there, is created an impact on us that tries to stop our desire of expressing our inner self, of unfolding our true person, our real soul. The cultural life, the state, the society, the family and all the powers that surround us seem to conspire to model and mould ourselves, to push us into their frames, to afflict us with their mechanical interest. We become part of a machine."

Children entering the educational system — some as young as two or three years of age — have no idea that they are spiritual beings made in the image and likeness of God and possess amazing powers and genius. Most likely, their parents, too, do not know the true identity of their children — or their own. Children's tender and impressionable souls become willing, trusting sponges that soak up information, wanting only to be loved and approved of, and they are taught by the system of reward and punishment. For this reason, whatever they learn in their most formative years becomes their core beliefs, through which they perceive life and make all their decisions. Later on, when the child as a teenager or adult is told something new that contradicts what she has learned, even if it is the truth, she will not believe it, unless she has awakened from her formerly dormant state and has activated her divine logic and vision. Home schooling gives us the opportunity to protect our children, to have direct control over what they learn, how they are treated, and which children and other people they associate with. Why let your child associate with disturbed and rivalrous children who have been dumbed down, repressed, and mentally and emotionally, perhaps even physically, abused?

Some people like giving others a piece of their confused and deluded minds. But it is our choice whether we listen and how we respond, or if we respond at all. Our awareness of the state of mind and motives of the people we live with, read about, watch on television or the Internet, or do business with gives us the upper hand, so that we cannot be fooled or misled.

Remember, there are people who want your vote, your soul power of manifestation, which you give when you agree with what they are saying and proposing. Voting does not happen only in the voting booth: we also vote with every dollar we spend and our every word, thought, and action. Stalin, the Russian dictator and murderer of millions, said that voters do not have the power, the ones who count the votes have the power. We vote by our consent, our agreement — by either buying or rejecting what others are selling, including their ideas, rules, laws, solutions, and prophecies. For those who would manipulate us, no cost is too high if it frightens us enough to make us give our allegiance to wolves in sheep's clothing.

This is how any abuser acts. People can say and do anything, but it is up to each of us to discern if what others are saying and doing is in alignment with spiritual truths based on love and the happiness and well-being of everyone, not just a few at the expense of the many. There is always enough for everyone when there is harmony and balance in nature, and we can create balance in the outer world by being balanced, by being centered in our hearts, rather than in our minds. We must recognize that anyone who uses fear, threats, force, or violence on anyone, any animal, or the planet is dangerous and up to no good. Withdraw your vote, and the person is left with only one vote — his.

But there is no need to hate such people, because when we hate them we take on their hateful, heavy, and depressing vibrations and must suffer the consequences. Have compassion for them — from a distance, for they have been conditioned and are hurting. Criticisms, judgments, and false information may come from their mouths, but this is their problem and not ours, unless we react from fear instead of acting as we choose from love. We must always be happy, for this is our job. We are the bliss of the world, and it is time to turn up the volume and the bliss vibration. As Robert Louis Stevenson said, "Every heart that has beat strong and cheerfully has left a hopeful impulse behind it in the world, and bettered the tradition of mankind."

The key to staying on course is to recognize that, while we may not know what others are going to do, we can always choose what we will do. Most people are reactors, always reacting to what is happening, with no idea why it is happening or that they have a choice in the matter. The best way to shield ourselves from difficulties that other people might try to cause for us is to cleanse our mind of all negativity, fear, and scarcity-based programming, regardless of where we learned it. Jesus advised us to be as little children, with fresh, clean minds and soft hearts. Take command of your mind and what you believe and act on: "Be not conformed to this world, but be ye transformed by the renewing of your mind, that ye might prove what is that good and perfect will of God" (Romans 12:2).

By understanding how our mind functions when it is focused on the outer world and thus fear of lack, we can understand why others do unkind things. Miserable people take pleasure in causing others pain but whatever they give out must and will come back to haunt them, as this is the law of reciprocity or cause and effect.

TAKING ADVICE

Once there was a village weaver who found that his loom had broken. He went to the forest to find some wood to fix it. He was about to cut down a tree when he heard the voice of a genie who lived in the hollow of the tree. "Kind sir," said the genie, if you spare the tree, which is my home, I will grant you any wish you desire."

The weaver was elated. He said to the genie, "Please wait a short while as I get some advice about what would be the best thing for me to ask you for."

When the weaver consulted his best friend, the man advised, "Ask for a kingdom, and then you will have everything you could ever need or want."

This sounded good to the weaver. On his way to tell the genie his decision, he met the village carpenter, who was known to have an envious streak. The carpenter advised, "You do not want a kingdom, for in a kingdom there are too many problems, which you will have to deal with. What you really need are two more arms and hands so you can make more fabrics and thus make more money. That's what I would ask for, and so would any intelligent person."

Convinced by what the carpenter said, and wanting to appear intelligent, the weaver told the genie in the tree of his decision. Immediately the weaver had two more arms and hands. Unfortunately, on his way home, some villagers spotted him and thought he was either a monster or an alien from another world and ran him out of town while beating him with sticks.

The lesson of this story is: When you listen to the advice of others, don't follow it blindly. We must consider three things: the motive of the advice giver; whether we really want to do what we are advised to do; and what the ramifications of our taking their advice will be. Others will tell us what to do, but we, not they, will suffer or enjoy the consequences of our actions.

Remember that you can be, do, and have whatever you choose, for all is possible within the All That Is Possible. The only limitations are the limitations of your thoughts. Our continual opportunity is to trust our inner guidance, our hearts' desires instead of our minds. We are to live from our hearts and use our minds to help us attain what we desire, not determine whether we can. When we recognize that there is a Higher Power always ready to help us by means of supernatural powers, life becomes an amazing adventure as the right people, situations, information, and resources come to us as if by magic. But it is not magic; it is real.

However, if you change your mind for any reason and take on the thought that you cannot do what must be done, or that it's not possible, then in the same way that digging up a carrot seed will kill the plant, you will stop your desire from manifesting and instead will get what you settled for. Thoughts are seeds, and all seeds will grow when believed. Open your mind to the All That Is Possible and select the thoughts that you want to manifest and release the others.

Some people will tell you that you cannot do the work you love because you cannot prosper while doing it, but this is the best and most enjoyable way to prosper, as you will discover in the next chapter.

Happiness and Prosperity Practices

A. Observe whether you are allowing anyone or anything to control, limit, repress, or discourage you from being true to yourself, expressing your talents fully, and living as you choose. Observe whether you have been trying to limit others. Observe whether you have any beliefs that are limiting you, or past experiences that you are using to limit yourself. If you have been doing any of these things, ask yourself why. Are you willing to shift your perception to the spiritual and transcendental platform and perceive your unlimited opportunities to prosper? Are you willing to allow your creative genius to flow through your heart and intelligence?

B. Contemplate the origin of all you can see around you, whether made by nature or humans. How many ideas do you perceive? Use the following declarations: Today,

I realize that I am as powerful as every other soul. Today, I recognize the creative power of my thoughts and emotions. Today, I make the habit of asking God Within for what I want to know and for what I desire to manifest.

C. Act as if you are as you desire to be, and you will be: Lift your awareness above any fear- and lack-based thoughts to the transcendental platform of all possibilities. Instead of wondering what others are thinking about you, know that what they are thinking of you is none of your business. Practice keeping your mind peaceful and centered at the third eye, and perceive the cause behind all creations: you and God.

Prospering Mantras

With God all things are possible.
Anything I desire is possible for me to experience.
I am a creative genius.
Divine Mind is now flowing through my mind.
All that I desire desires me.

CHAPTER FOUR

Prosper and Live Blissfully
by Doing What You Love

You and I are prosperity, so we don't need to work for money or go to a job to make it. The Federal Reserve and governments make money at the mint, not us. Nine out of ten people whose purpose in business is to make money, lose money. U.S. money still has "In God We Trust" printed on it, both paper bills and coins. Read this every time you use this form of money to remind yourself of where your prosperity, power, and security come from.

Working for God makes us rich spiritually and materially and also happy, because we are human beings, souls with feeling bodies, not cold, inert machines. *Soul satisfaction is generated in the process of contribution, in helping others to be happy, healthy, and prosperous.* When money and power are our motivators, then we will exploit people in order to benefit ourselves, instead of working for their welfare. The secret of a successful business and a happy life is in service — in giving of our talents, abilities, and whatever else we have produced that will help others and contribute to their well-being.

Giving is our nature as children of God, for God is the ulti-mate giver, the master of contribution. "As above, so below" tells us who we are and how we function. Because our eternal nature is godlike, we are also contributors, givers. Everyone has some-thing to give in exchange for what each wants to receive. By the law of nature called *circulation*, as we give what others need and desire, we will also receive what we need and desire. But if we are not offering our goods and services — not exchanging what others desire for what we desire — how can there be an exchange of money or goods and services?

We must give to receive and receive to give — this is how the system works. Once we understand how the cycle of prosperity operates, we simply get busy engaging in our life's work. First we need to know and believe that we are enough. This is a constant. All souls are enough, and each of us possesses enough to start the process of generating prosperity, the flow of opulence. When we do this, besides what we gain materially, we experience satisfac-tion, fulfillment, and joy. What is prosperity other than the faith and impetus to go forward with our plans with enthusiasm?

Unfortunately, many people make money their source and prosperity, and when they believe they do not have enough money to do what they want, they give up. Nothing is worse than not fol-lowing our heart or doing our life's work, because our enthusi-asm and joy in living diminishes. What every person needs to know is that she has enough to go forward with her plans. And starting and continuing, even if this means taking the tiniest baby steps, guarantee that she will arrive at her desired destination while having a lovely time all the way.

Money is a tool we use. Money does not create our prosper-ity; we do, through our soul power, the power to cocreate, the power behind our desires and natural genius to manifest what we need and want. It's never really about the paper, gold, silver, and promissory notes — since what is needed and wanted is not these, as you cannot eat or drink them — it's about what we can exchange the money for. Money in reserve is for obtaining future pleasures and needs. But sometimes people lose their savings and investments, or these are devalued. By understanding this from the spiritual perspective, we can see that, when money or someone we were depending upon for the future fails us, it's an opportunity to remember, and turn back to, the Higher Power, our eternal Source and supply. When people lose their investments or savings or whatever they were depending on to provide for their future needs and pleasures, does this mean they will starve or not be able to live a happy and satisfying life? No! Usually it means that the person has more to give and, instead of giving, was simply trying to survive and enjoy life.

We are prosperity, as I said before, and we need to remember this. You and I and every other soul are the life force that animates dull matter. We create it and activate it so that it functions. In the same way that God is ultimate prosperity — possessing everything that exists anywhere — and the Supreme Creator, we too are creators who are always manifesting things through our thoughts, words, feelings, and deeds, in a way that does not depend on the current form of money. If the current money system does not serve us, we can bypass it and create another form of exchange. Or we can go direct and simply trade products and services; better yet, we can operate on the human level of giving and receiving as loving members of one family helping each other.

Working for money makes money our boss, whereas working for love makes love our boss. Thinking that you are working to make money is not correct. Money is supposed to be working for us so we can use it in our service to God and others. Only the federal government is in the business of printing money, and only moneychangers (the bankers) are in the business of using money as a product. Saying that we are going to work to make money is not the best way to think about our work. We are children of God engaged in the family business, which is working for the welfare of others — helping others to be happy, healthy, and prosperous. There is nothing right or wrong with having money; money is neither good nor bad, it just is. Money does not create or solve our problems; we do.

The secret of a successful business is to help others get what they want and solve their problems. When getting money is the purpose of our work, we constantly feel stress and remain worried about the lack of money. On the other hand, if large sums of money come to us, then we may worry about preventing their loss. Had I not learned how to manifest what I wanted when I didn't have much money, I would have thought money was the source of my prosperity. Using the principle of investment, I invested my time and resources in educating myself spiritually and developing my talents and skills. At first I thought I wanted money because I thought money would give me freedom. Soon I realized I was already free to do what I wanted. Whenever I desired to attain something, I used the steps of manifestation, and it came to me — sometimes instantly and effortlessly, sometimes as a result of my spending money, sometimes in the form of a gift, and sometimes as a prize for winning a contest. The more I engaged in doing my life's work of helping others with my knowledge and talents, the more fortunate I became and the more I prospered. Once you start, doors open that had been closed before.

There is an abundance of all things, including love, bliss, money, time, energy, and ideas, to name a few. We live in a sea of inexhaustible divine energy waiting to be expressed through us by our thoughts, desires, and deeds. This abundance is available to anyone who seeks it and taps into its limitless supply. But we have to choose to tap into it. Even God cannot force anyone to prosper or be happy. Our work is to be aware of and accept this abundance prepared for us at the foundation of the universe. The Creator is the source of a mighty stream of substance, and we are tributaries, channels of expression. In the same way that water circulates throughout the earthly system by the process of giving and receiving, abundance can circulate through us when we go with the flow.

Circulation Is the Principle of Prosperity

The soil brings forth trees and plants that give us food. Sunshine gives us light, warmth, and energy. Cows give us milk from which we can produce butter, cheese, yogurt, and even ice cream. Flowers give us fragrance and beauty. All this tells us that our mission, too, is to give, to contribute to others.

In order to give, we must also receive by allowing others to give to us. Giving and receiving are two sides of the same coin, two parts of one system. For example, when we plant a fruit or nut tree and make sure that it gets water, nutrients, and protection from critters, and is placed in a location where it receives ample sunlight, the tree will give us a bountiful crop to enjoy and nourish the body. But if we plant the tree and ignore it, it may die, and it definitely will not flourish as it could have with the proper love and care. This system of reciprocation is at work in our personal and business relationships too.

Jesus's parable about talents is a perfect analogy of how the law of prosperity works for one and all. He said, "For unto every one that hath shall be given, and he shall have abundance: but from him that hath not shall be taken away even that which he hath" (Matthew 25:29). Jesus also said, "Give and it shall be given unto you" (Luke 6:38). These verses explain how the abundant flow of divine opulence and bliss operate. Giving is the activity of love, and miserliness is the activity of fear of lack and the cause of misery.

Similarly, the fifth Hermetic axiom states that everything flows in and out. And according to Eastern wisdom, a form of God named Vishnu, who sits with the Goddess of Fortune, Laxmi, by his side, brings forth the creation when he exhales, and he brings it all back into his body when he inhales. This is a continual process of outflow and inflow, giving and receiving. And being mentally and emotionally open to receiving the divine flow of opulence from God is always the first step. Then when we give — even if we give only a little at first but consistently continue to offer our talents, goods, and services — we will consistently have more to give, for we consistently receive more.

Receiving Means Knowing That We Have Enough to Begin the Prosperity Process

Therefore keep the words of this covenant, and do them, that you may prosper in all that you do.

DEUTERONOMY 29:9

Once we learn how the law of prosperity works, and we are aware of God's unlimited abundance, we can set out on the road to personal riches. Repeatedly hearing and reading about this unlimited abundance helps us to remember what is always available to us regardless of the world's condition. We must raise our awareness to the spiritual zone, where we are free of the filters created by our prejudices and fear- and lack-based mental conditioning. When we open our minds to the possibilities beyond our current resources, we are able to receive help from the Supernatural, which is never limited by worldly conditions. For example, when I first started my work as a motivational speaker, media people were, in some mystical way, inspired to write great articles about my work, giving me millions of dollars' worth of free publicity. I didn't have a public relations firm, nor was I seeking to pay for PR, as I didn't have that much money. Doors opened to me because my intention was strong, and I knew that a power greater than I was helping me just as this power had helped others before me.

Give up the fixed-income, fixed-situation, and no-possibility mentality. Give up the idea that what you want to do will cost you a fortune, or that you cannot do it because you do not have enough money or aren't good enough. A woman I recently met made a fabulous movie for only ten thousand dollars. People came forward and volunteered their talents, time, and equipment because they believed in the value of her work. Your job may determine your salary, but not your income. Income comes from God, as does everything else, so keep your mind open and what you want and need will come to you. You may not yet have the resources you believe you need, but do not limit yourself by thinking you won't get them, because your thoughts will be made manifest. We regulate how much or how little of the flow of energy we experience by how much we are willing to receive from all avenues, all possible rivers and streams of income: money, gifts, and opportunities.

We Are Enough

The thought that we are not deserving, not good enough, or that there isn't enough of whatever we need to thrive discourages people who believe these lies. In my counseling work, I found that most of my clients' number one concern was the belief that they were not capable enough or deserving enough to get or keep the relationships or career positions they desired, or to prosper. With such beliefs, we can never get enough, be enough, or do enough to please others or to feel good, because the conditioned mind reminds us that we are not enough, not good enough to be loved and wanted. One of my colleagues shared with me her memory that, from the time she was a young girl, until the time she was grown and she left home, her mother would frequently say to her, "What is wrong with you?" Her mother would say to others, too: "What is wrong with this girl?" My colleague is a beautiful person in every way and highly intelligent, so it is strange that her mother would speak of her as if she were flawed.

Believing that we lack beauty, intelligence, social position, wealth, and talent, that we are not as good as others, is painful and grossly limiting and it's not true. This is just one example of how the conditioned mind can destroy people's lives. What my colleague's mother told her was not true, and is not true about anyone, ever. Making our life's purpose about proving our worth as a person is pathetic and a waste of our precious opportunity as a human being. Our endeavors to prove that we are good enough, or even better than others, only serve to invalidate our value in our own minds, because no matter what we do, we will still feel unworthy until we understand the lie and give it up by realizing our perfection as godlike souls. When our core belief is "I am not enough," this becomes a self-fulfilling prophecy. Just drop it.

Affirm: I am enough and have always been enough. Dropping the concept "I am not good enough to be loved and approved of or to prosper" involves dropping our concern about what anyone, including our parents, children, and mate, thinks of us.

Forget Scarce Supply

Poverty thoughts must prove themselves right by manifesting as lack — the lack of customers, clients, friends, money, attention, appreciation, opportunities, time, energy, happiness, love, ideas, and so on. Even where there is an abundance of everything, nothing is good enough to satisfy the person who has poverty consciousness. He remains afraid, and runs as fast as he can to get more before it's all gone. It's common for businesses to run ads that say: hurry, buy now, there's a limited supply, don't be left out . . .

People with poverty consciousness can be dangerous. Thomas Malthus (1766–1834), a British economist, came up with the theory that there wasn't and wouldn't be enough food and resources for everyone. Remember that the general theory of economics is based on scarcity supply. The spiritual person recognizes that there is no scarcity. The concept fosters greed and competition and justifies wars and cruelty toward humans and animals. Malthus even proposed artificial population management of the masses by the leaders, who believed they were superior to others and that it was their job to control everyone and everything. On the other hand, Buckminster Fuller — an American engineer, inventor, designer, architect, educator, poet, and philosopher well known for his technology designed to deal with global problems — discovered that there are enough natural renewable resources for every man, woman, and child to have over four million dollars a year to spend for life. The word *renewable* is the key to his work. He documented this in his book *Critical Path*, if you are interested in finding out more about his research. This does not sound like scarcity. His findings were about renewable natural resources and living in harmony with one another and nature.

The point is: earth is abundant, and so are we when we take care of the earth and each other. This happens to be our lesson: that we must work together in love. We must do our research and find out what is true instead of being led like sheep to go against our divine nature, which makes us feel bad and develop cruel ways of speaking and treating other humans and animals. With the poverty concept of scarce supply controlling us, we remain frightened about what will happen to us in the future. Remember that there is no greater terrorist weapon than our minds. Scarcity theories pervade the work climate and cause people to be cutthroat in order to destroy their so-called competition and ruin them by "making a killing" — interesting words to use in business.

Our work may appear to be the production and distribution of goods and services, but really our work is love, helping people. We are human beings, not impersonal machines without feelings, and so are our clients and customers. How can we express love and help people through our work in a way that also allows us to become happier and experience more love and sweetness? When money and power are the purpose of business, people are not important except as objects to exploit. However, when we understand that the purpose of business is to truly help people, then our hearts soften and our work becomes satisfying, because we build relationships. When we use our work as another way to make a difference — by being kind, compassionate, and helpful to our customers, clients, and students — our work becomes more fulfilling for us.

I teach my students that we are all ministers, and that our work, whatever it is, is our ministry, our opportunity to teach our philosophy by our example. We teach it through the way we speak, what we say, how we treat others, the kinds of products and services we offer, the songs we sing or roles we play in movies if we are entertainers, our attitudes, and the gifts we give in the form of writings and recordings that inspire and encourage others. We help people by allowing God's love to be expressed through us and everything we do. There is no need to preach or be a fanatic: we just need to be living examples of the philosophy and spiritual teachings we believe. This is our greatest challenge, no matter what happens in the world or is projected to happen: being who we are as human beings, the children of Mother/Father God on a mission of love and compassion.

Working for Love

A prosperous person is one whose life is about contribution, for she is rich in friends, family, and clients, and rich in heart and soul. Most of us spend the majority of our time doing our work. Why shouldn't we do the work we love with love and enthusiasm in the mood of service? Spiritually enlivened people live their bliss by doing what they love, which suits their nature and character. By doing what we love, we never have to work another day in our lives. I never wanted a job; I wanted a life's work. How boring to have merely a job. When I did have a job in high school, before I understood about the mood of service and contribution, I would get so bored and would watch the clock, counting the hours until I could go home.

How wonderful to be engaged in meaningful work we enjoy that also offers us the freedom to do what we want and have a lifestyle designed around our life's work. Working for love, we have the power of the Divine behind us: it is the wind beneath our wings, and it goes ahead of us to clear the path of obstacles. When we have a spiritual purpose greater than simply having a job to pay our bills and make ends meet, our options and possibilities for fulfillment, money, and even fame increase.

Purpose

For a man to achieve all that is demanded of him,
he must regard himself as greater than he is.

JOHANN WOLFGANG VON GOETHE

Purpose gives us the focus, direction, and overriding reason for our existence. Another way to understand purpose is to envision it as a basket, as the context that holds the content of our lives, including our goals, lifestyles, activities, relationships, and businesses. Purpose never ends. It's like a river that keeps flowing and carrying the boat we travel on; goals are like the stops we make while on the journey, and they are complete once we reach them. When each goal is accomplished, we continue down the river to our next objective. Everything fits together, everything is flowing in the same river, which increases the power we have to work with, for we have a single vision, purpose, and plan. Our mission is our passionate desire to help others by our presence and by how we treat them, as well as by the products and services we offer them.

Once we know our purpose and mission, then it's easy to set our goals and know where we want to live, the people to associate with, and how we can use our talents, knowledge, and resources to help others. When we don't know our purpose and mission, then we are simply stimulus-response machines reacting to other people and situations, instead of acting as we choose in a way that helps us attain what we desire. When we know our purpose, then we align our lives and our businesses along that path, and everything we do contributes to the attainment of our purpose, mission, and goals.

All our dreams, goals, and activities have a place in the basket of our grand purpose. Challenges, failures, successes, blessings, and difficulties — all contribute to our attaining this higher purpose, because we take whatever lessons come to us and apply them, instead of allowing them to discourage or defeat us. With a grand purpose, we welcome each valuable lesson as a missing piece we needed in order to succeed at the next step. Even a mistake of the sort that previously could have destroyed us is no longer a failure but a blessing. A grand purpose worthy of us eliminates obstacles, such as the glass ceiling that may have kept us down, and it exponentially expands our possibilities for expressing the genius in the form of potential that lies within us.

Our highest purpose is simply to love God, the reservoir of bliss, love, beauty, and opulence, which allows us to attain God-consciousness. With God-consciousness all things are possible, for what could be more exalted than having the consciousness of God?

Mission

Our mission, as children of God, is to help all souls, all creatures great and small to be happy, healthy, and prosperous. Whatever God is doing is what we are meant to do. God is love, so we are love. God is bliss, so we are bliss. God is always working for the welfare of everyone; therefore, we are to work for the welfare of others and not exploit or abuse them. Our mission is to be God's representatives in the world, the hands and spiritual presence that elevates the predominant frequency of humanity from the lower levels of violence to bliss. All of God's creations have the right to live out their lives in peace and happiness without being tormented by misdirected humans.

Our job description is contained in the following scripture: "And God made the beasts of the earth after their kind, and the cattle after their kind, and everything that creeps upon the earth after its kind; and God saw that it was good. Then God said, Let us make man in our image, after our likeness; and let them have dominion over the fish of the sea, and over the fowl of the air, and over the cattle and over all the wild beasts of the earth, and over every creeping thing that creeps upon the earth" (Genesis 2:25–26). *Dominion* means "authority." It is not about lording it over others, abusing them, or causing them distress, and this includes animals. In the same way that a caretaker of a great and opulent estate and gardens is able to enjoy all the benefits and bounty within them, we are supplied with all that we need when we engage in our mission by undertaking our right livelihood.

Products and Services to Offer

A person who has mastered the self and who strives
by right means is assured of success.

EASTERN WISDOM

To engage in right livelihood means to support ourselves while offering products and services that are good for the body, mind, and soul. Whatever we like to do, and whatever talents, skills, and knowledge we have, we can be of service to others. There is always someone who would like to receive what we know. Our valuable experiences, propensities, and talents can be made into life-affirming services and products that are good for Mother Earth and all her flora and fauna.

Ask yourself, "What services and products can I offer in order to help more people be happy, get what they want, and prosper?" Make a list of all the products and services that you can offer, given your education, expertise, propensities, and talents. What would you really like to do if you could do anything at all?

For example, if you love to garden, then your method for serving humanity could be growing and selling plants or doing something else related to gardening. You can create a lifestyle around gardening — or whatever else you love to do. Perhaps you love to travel. If so, then make travel your business by offering travel-related services and products. You'll be able to make money and, at the same time, live as you choose, instead of working at another job in order to get enough money to travel. Do what you love, do what resonates in your soul — your life's work — and the money and whatever else you need in order to do your work and live as you choose will come to you.

Once we decide what we have to offer in the way of goods and services, then we can think about our goals — when, where, and how we will offer what we have to others. Once we set our goals and make our agreements, it's important to keep our word as best we can by delivering what we have promised, in order to cultivate both prosperity and trust. Delivery means the opportunity to exchange the money we earn for what we want, but no delivery, no money.

Be True to Yourself All the Time

As soon as you trust yourself, you will know how to live.

JOHANN WOLFGANG VON GOETHE

While trust is important for building a successful business, trusting ourselves is even more important, especially when it comes to our life's work. Avoid allowing others, no matter who they are, to coerce you into pursuing a business that does not suit you or give you pleasure. Geniuses are people who follow their bliss. They must be who they are and do the work that thrills their soul — anything else is painful, since souls are not machines but spiritual beings on a mission of self-evolution and expression. The Bhagavad Gita states, "It is better to discharge one's own work, even if faulty, than another's work perfectly." The importance of being true to oneself has been taught throughout time.

Sometimes, as a stopgap measure, we need to take work that is not what we really like, but this can yield a blessing. We can use the opportunity to learn something about this type of work and can develop a good attitude about service. Whatever our work, it's most important to be enthusiastic about it while performing it with love, all the while keeping in mind that our real work is giving and receiving love, not stuff — not things made of molecules — or power over others.

Generate Prosperity by the Power of Love

Love is the most powerful driving emotion, and it makes all things possible for us to attain. All people are driven by emotions, some by anger, rivalry, greed, or hatred, and others by love of people, work, and God. Those traveling the prosperity road are always thinking about how to better serve their clients, students, customers, friends, and family members. Once we realize that all souls are our family members, we treat all with respect and have compassion for them. We receive our happiness when God is happy expressing through us.

A mother's love increases with every thought about her child's welfare and happiness. Her child's happiness is her happiness. Motherly love is the closest thing to the love that God feels for us. Mothers, however, are not the only ones who can feel motherly love: it is what we need to strive for in all our dealings and relationships, in our personal lives and businesses. Of course, we do not treat others as helpless infants, nor do we serve them in the same way that we care for our children, but all souls are God's precious children. One of my friends related a story about a time when he was meditating at a holy temple in India. He said to God, "What do you want me to do?" A voice inside replied, "Chant and dance and love everyone as I do." This will sound strange to someone who has been programmed to believe that singing and dancing are for fools. A skeptical person such as this wastes her entire life struggling to attain things, power, and prestige, when these come to us naturally when we are happily doing our life's work.

Some people work because they love their work. Some work because they love people, animals, or Mother Earth. Theists work with love and devotion for the pleasure of God. When we work for the love of God, we are also working for the welfare of all, because tending to the welfare of all souls, including animals, is God's work. Generate as much affection as you can for your clients, customers, Mother Earth, and others, regardless of race, religion, nationality, sex, and species, and then you will always feel good. Your job is to remember that you, as the bliss of the world, are on a mission of love.

How to Actualize Prosperity

Do the thing and the power is yours; don't do it and you don't have the power. Unless we turn the ignition key on — that is, unless we do something — the automobile sits there in the ready mode but can't take us to our destination. You can stand in an elevator all day, but it won't go anywhere until you push the button for the floor you want.

I have witnessed people who affirm prosperity over and over but don't experience an increase in their money or good fortune, only because they are not producing and offering products and services. This teaching works when we work it. A piano doesn't make us a skilled pianist — we must play it. Prosperity thoughts, affirmations, and mantras get us to the door of the treasure house of spiritual and material riches, but to open the door we must use the key of action. In my early days of learning how to prosper, I entered contests, raffles, and such and won. If I hadn't taken the action of entering the contest, how could I have won? I counted my winnings as unexpected income. Winnings don't take the place of our life's work, which is most important for our self-expression and long-range prospering. The point is to be open to receiving expected and unexpected streams of income, gifts, and opportunities. A life's work is much more than just a way to receive money: it is our role and place in the grand scheme of things and our avenue for bringing forth our genius and making a difference.

"Whosoever will be great among you, let him or her minister unto the people's needs; and whosoever will be chief among you, let him or her give service in that field in which he or she is most skilled" (Matthew 20:26–27). This statement of Jesus is the formula for success in our careers. Ministering to the needs of others and offering services in the fields in which we are most skilled are the most important teachings of business.

Wishful thinking does not serve others. It's mainly about what we will get, rather than what we can give. Until we become absorbed in the process of contributing to the welfare of others, all we have are wishes and shattered dreams. Once we activate and set in motion the opulent flow of divine energy by offering our knowledge, expertise, and life-enhancing products, then the floodgates open and all sorts of expected and unexpected gifts, money, and opportunities start flowing to us. If we stop giving or receiving, we experience stagnation.

Start Now with What You Have

Whatever you can do, or dream you can, begin it.
Boldness has genius, power, and magic in it.

JOHANN WOLFGANG VON GOETHE

Do it, now. Stop waiting for a better time or for when you have more money, your bills are all paid, your children are grown, you lose weight, get a boyfriend or husband, the economy is better, or there is peace in the world. Start doing what you love as your life's work. Do what generates your sweet feelings and creates a space for others to also feel good. Begin to offer your goods and services.

A giant redwood tree starts as a tiny seed planted in fertile soil. It is activated by water, which is called the semen of God in Vedic teachings. Start now, and every day do your work by offering your goods and services. Sing your song, make the clothes and jewelry, help others with their projects, and so on. We all have enough of whatever is needed to begin going forward with our plans. Start with what you have. Even if you must begin in the most infinitesimally small way, forward movement is the catalyst that opens doors. There is no better time than now, for all things great and small can happen only in this moment.

Getting ready can consume a lifetime if we let it. My philosophy is: fire, ready, aim. Begin. Then the power starts flowing and the process of manifestation is activated. You will learn on the way. Always preparing for, but never doing the thing, is a sign of fear and faith in failure. The musician who is always wondering what will happen if he fails, hides his talents, kills his dreams, and focuses on merely surviving, instead of offering his music to the greatest number of people for their enjoyment and spiritual enlightenment.

We have all heard the instruction that if you are going to do something, then do it right or don't do it at all. This doesn't even make sense. We wouldn't tell a child not to try to walk unless she can walk perfectly the first time, without falling down. What is failure, other than simply not attempting to do what it is we want to do? There are always the naysayers, the critics who are hoping to see you fail because they are envious. They seek pleasure from the pain of others as if they will then find the happiness they seek. We can only get what we want from its source — and all pleasures of the soul come from the reservoir of pleasure, God. Do the thing, and the power is yours to succeed. Don't do it, and it won't happen. Whatever you offer, offer it with love, the greatest motivating and actualizing power that exists.

Distributing Our Services or Products
to as Many People as Possible

When we believe in our products and services, naturally we want to distribute them to as many people as possible because of the benefits that others will receive. Make a list of the benefits, and describe the value, of what you are offering so that you are certain what these are. Are you willing to receive money or whatever else you desire in exchange for what you are offering? Money is part of the exchange for goods and services, and business is regulated by supply and demand — this is natural. Unless there is production and distribution — unless we offer our talents, goods, and services — how can there be an inflow of money, goods, and services? Communicate with your potential customers and clients and share with them the value and benefits they will receive from taking you up on your offers. Make sure you accept that it is perfectly right for you to prosper by doing what you love.

Happiness and Prosperity Practices

A. Observe how you feel about your job and career and whether it suits you. Observe when you feel envious of someone else's career, work, or talent, as this will help you know more about what you want to be doing. Observe if you are willing to prosper from the distribution of your products and services and the offering of your talents. Remember all the activities that you have done that you really enjoy.

B. Contemplate what gives you the greatest satisfaction and pleasure and then write a list of all the products and services you could offer from these activities. What service or product would you offer if you did not need money and you had the freedom to do whatever you choose? Use the following declarations: Today, I will do my work with love for the benefit of my clients and customers. Today, I will feel grateful for whatever work I have and be kind to my customers and clients. Today, I will realize that there are millions of people who can benefit from my talents, goods, and services.

C. Act as if you are as you desire to be, and you will be: associate with people who are manifesting the consciousness, talents, and life's work that you desire, and learn from them. Remember: consciousness is contagious. Start with whatever you have, no matter how little, and begin to offer your talents, products, and services to the greatest possible number of people who can benefit. Remember: do the work and the power is yours to be successful, but if you don't there is nothing to exchange.

Prospering Mantras

I am prosperity.

It is perfectly right for me to prosper doing the work I enjoy.

I have enough to begin offering my talents, products, and services to others.

I have a vast amount of love, resources, and creativity available to me.

CHAPTER FIVE

Pleasure-Producing Relationships

*A*ll relationships can be pleasurable when we know how to generate happiness regardless of what others say and do. Love and prosperity are self-generated because we are love and prosperity. Because we are love, we do not and cannot get love from anyone, but when we are around people who like us, it is easier to be ourselves (which is love). Once we are Self-realized, we are in a constant state of love. We are being ourselves under any and all circumstances even when others dislike or disapprove of us. The main problem in relationships is the belief that we must have the approval of others and their undying devotion and commitment before we can be happy and secure enough to be ourselves without the fear of rejection, loss, or abandonment. Love is not a thing or a commodity that we must pay for or be afraid of losing. It may appear that other people are the cause of our happiness or distress, but this is not true. We are the cause of our happiness or distress.

What we want are mutually supportive relationships where

each person is a winner and can bring forth the greatness that is within her or him and not feel suppressed, coerced, bad, or guilty for mistakes or successes. Souls want to have loving relationships with other souls. Most of what people experience in relationships has been based on concepts passed down from generation to generation from religion and cultural conditioning and has nothing to do with the real purpose of relationships, which is bliss. Soul-to-soul relationships are real and deeply satisfying because we can be ourselves without fear. Offering another the gift of unconditional love is the greatest gift we can give another. There are seven actions that lead to our becoming a master in the art of rewarding relationships even if, in the past, some of our relationships have been troublesome. They are:

1. Accept that every soul, including our own, is pure goodness and perfect without flaws of any kind.

2. Assume responsibility for our own feelings and actions as well as for the results we are getting.

3. Understand that others are the cause of their own emotions and actions as well as the cause of the results they are getting.

4. Be willing for others to be happy, prosperous, and successful in their endeavors and for us to be happy, prosperous, and successful in our endeavors.

5. Treat all others with respect and honor their freedom to be, do, and have what they choose as we also honor ourselves and our freedom to be, do, and have what we choose.

6. Be kind to all living entities, speak sweet words, and seek to be a beacon of inspiration, enthusiasm, and encouragement to all.

7. Recognize that the way we are treating others is the way we are treating ourselves because what we give out is what we will get back.

The heart of the matter when it comes to successful relationships is accepting that every soul including us is pure goodness and perfect without flaws of any kind. The common approach has been to find fault in others because we believe that we ourselves are flawed and thus bad and wrong. No one likes to feel bad or not good enough to be loved and accepted so the habit of finding fault in others has made us feel at least better than others. How can we be happy in our relationships when we harbor the thought that there is something wrong with us? We often judge a person's actions toward us based on our expectations. An insecure person is in constant need of reassurance as to her worth to another and in constant anxiety over the possible loss of the relationship. Our minds will calculate the words and actions of others to mean that there is something wrong with us, and that they do not love us or else they would behave as we expect. When our self-worth is based on the opinion of another person, we set ourselves up for pain.

Even in relationships that start out well, familiarity can breed contempt when one or both of the people are not happy and then blame the other and find fault in the other person. What happened? Not even God can make us feel good all the time unless we seek out the cause of our distress, which is self-alienation. No one will ever be good enough in our minds until we know that we are good enough, that we are perfect just as we are. Once we really know this, then our actions are motivated by love and kindness. The medicine that heals the disease of "not good enough" is to bypass everything that we have heard or been taught that gave us the idea that something is wrong with us and therefore we are not good enough to be loved by God, our parents, relatives, mates, and others. This is all fear and lack-based conditioning and not true about anyone.

Once we stop judging others as not good enough and stop criticizing others in order to feel better about ourselves, the "not good enough" program running in our subconscious will fade and disappear for lack of faith. You do not need to prove anything to anyone in order for you to feel good; feel good because you are pure goodness. We are not here on earth to seek the approval of others, and we already have God's love and approval. Accept it and forget all the soap opera stories of who did what to you and when.

God Is Our Primary Relationship

Our first relationship is with our Creator, our Source. All relationships spring from this primary relationship. The more we build and enjoy our primary relationship with God, the sweeter life becomes and the more satisfying our other relationships become. If we believe that God does not love us or that God is punishing us, we will also believe that others do not love us and are punishing us. Thinking we are not good enough to be loved by God, we will also believe that our parents do not love us, nor do others. Projecting the image of our earthly parents onto our Divine Eternal Parents, Mother/Father God will cause us to believe that our Divine Parents are like our earthly parents even though this is not true at all. For example, a person with abusive parents will believe that God is abusive and will hate God. Yet God is kind, sweet, and devoted to us. Unless we have spiritual vision, we will project the way our parents treated us onto all others. If we did not get the love we wanted from our mothers, we will be dissatisfied in our relationships with women, and if we disliked our father or he wasn't there when we needed him, we will place all men in this category. When that happens, a person's life becomes centered around unsatisfactory primary relationships. Feeling bad just to prove how bad others were to us isn't very intelligent. Instead, we can have as much love as we are willing to feel regardless of what did or did not happen in the past.

Think of a circle with your God in the center like the sun. Warmth comes from the sun just as whatever we need and desire must come from a source that possesses whatever we need and want. When we understand that God is our center, our Soul and the Soul of every soul, as well as the Higher Power, then if one person does not give us what we want, another person, who has been inspired by our mutual Supersoul to do this, will.

The basis of all enriching relationships is accepting personal responsibility rather than handing over the responsibility for our feelings and prosperity to others, which will always set us up for disappointment and arguments. The main source of arguments and disappointments is unfulfilled expectations. They lead to comments like: "I thought this is what you would do, but you didn't," "I didn't know this is what you expected me to do," "You never do what I want you to do," "You really don't love me. If you loved me, then you would have . . . ," "I never feel like I am enough for you," or "You are not treating me the way I expected to be treated."

The higher purpose of any relationship is spiritual advancement by learning and practicing the art of unconditional love. Even the most difficult situation can be used to attain great benefits when we seek to sustain our feelings of unconditional love instead of falling into despair and resentment. Of course no one needs to stay in an abusive relationship, but the test is to keep the mind situated on the spiritual, transcendental plane. We are not our stories or dreams, we are spiritual beings with the power of choice to act and feel as we choose regardless of what is going on in the world. From this higher level of perception, we perceive people as souls who are exercising their free will by their choices and who can change those choices at any moment. Few people know this so they continue on their quest for happiness by blaming others for their problems and lack of whatever it is they want but aren't getting.

We can work together with others in mutually supportive situations, but not dump the responsibility for what happens to us on them or feel guilty for their self-generated problems. Although we can do our best to help others, we are not God. Unless we want to carry the weight of the world upon our shoulders, we must understand this: Each person is exactly where he or she needs to be for whatever lessons that person requires. Once that lesson has been learned, that situation will disappear and the next situation for the next lesson will appear.

Agreements Build Relationships

We have a better chance for our personal and business relationships to be mutually beneficial when there is a higher purpose. These relationships work best when each person sincerely wants and strives to use the relationship to make spiritual progress, develop unconditional love, and to attain worldly prosperity. Creating basic agreements will help each person to remember and attain the higher spiritual purpose for the partnership. These guidelines will help bring forth the divine, godlike nature of each individual as well as genius and talents.

Unless we have some agreements that make our relationships

a safe harbor where we can grow spiritually and also develop relationship skills, we may simply keep on repeating old habits that only create problems. We tend to drag our beliefs, programming, and relationship baggage along with us into every relationship. Most of this is not valuable but a detriment to our having loving, reciprocal partnerships, and all relationships are partnerships. Because we are creatures of habit, we must make new habits when we realize that our old habits of thinking, speaking, and treating others are creating only conflict and alienation instead of closeness and trust. When we have mutually agreed-upon guidelines in our families, businesses, and communities, we are able to quickly solve disagreements and create a little heaven on earth. The agreements shown in the following list are only suggestions. Create your own to suit your purpose. Making your own agreements with the other members is a wonderful exercise because you learn something about each other, their desire and what contributions each are willing to make.

The list of mutual agreements can be posted on the wall and used in family or business meetings to clear the air and allow each person to share without feeling judged or made wrong and bad. We cannot force others into complying with our rules — force and intimidation do not breed success. We all like being around people who like us and who accept the perfection of our true, divine nature as a god. Aligning with others for a specific purpose or objective provides far more power for manifesting our objectives. "Again I say to you, that if two of you are worthy on earth, anything that they would ask, it will be done for them by my Father in heaven" (Matthew 18:19).

Here are suggested agreements for your family, business, or community to post:

1. I choose to remember to treat others in the manner that I would like to be treated.

2. I choose to be tolerant, compassionate, and encouraging.

3. If there is a problem, I will seek a solution that works for all involved.

4. I will be responsible for my feelings, actions, and results.

5. I will be straightforward, kind, and gentle in my communications.

6. I will take responsibility for my communications being understood.

7. I choose to remember that each person is a child of God and therefore a god with free will.

8. I choose to practice unconditional love and be a safe space where each person is able to share his or her thoughts, concerns, and desires.

9. I choose to enjoy the happiness and good fortune of all others and wish them well.

10. I choose to serve my God and others with love and affection for their happiness, and I respect the spiritual faith of others.

11. I choose to keep my agreements once they are made, and if I need to change an agreement I will do so in a responsible and timely manner.

12. When a mistake has been made, I will seek a solution without making anyone wrong or myself right.

13. I will create my own boundaries as to what works for me and support others in doing the same.

No One Owns Another

Each of us is free to live as we choose, even if we choose to be miserable, but no one has license to interfere with the right of other living entities to live in the way they choose. Likewise, parents do not own children; we are their guardians, protectors, teachers, and well-wishers. Our role is to help them to become God-realized, supreme human beings. Parents are caretakers of souls for God. We do not own the land, the animals, or anything else in this world, including pets. We are the caretakers, children of God on a mission of love. Thou shalt not kill or cause distress to any living entity, including animals, is a law of life. Each soul has a right to live out her eternal life as she chooses and advance in her evolution up the ladder to full Self-realization and self-actualization. I capitalize Self when it refers to Supersoul within and small when it is our individual self. Whatever we do to others, including any animal will be done to us through the laws of karma, so we can make the corrections and take our rightful place as gods in the grand scheme of things. Remember that Mother Earth is a school and not the final destination but a place where we are trained and prepared for our eternal place in the stars and beyond.

People are not chattel, no matter who makes the laws. Any law made that gives anyone including any government, corporation, or agency control of others is wrong and in violation of the universal prime directive of free will. Wives don't belong to husbands, and husbands are not the property of wives, nor are children the property of parents. All souls are sovereign and need to be perceived in this way. We are actually volunteers in each and every relationship or group. In order to have satisfying, pleasure-giving relationships, we must honor each person's sovereignty, as well as our own. The souls we call our children have their own paths too, just as we have ours. They come to us for the purpose of unconditional love and for no other reason.

Never imply that something is wrong with your child or punish them by abuse or threats of rejection. Talk with and explain and also allow them to receive the reactions of their actions so that they understand that basic law of nature — cause and effect — action and reaction. When we love someone, we do whatever we can to help them attain their purpose, life's mission, and goals, but we do not set these for them, they do. The guidelines we set up are to help our children to be successful human beings by understanding the basic laws of nature as well as their spiritual nature as a godlike soul possessing mystic powers of manifestation. Our purpose is to shelter and protect our children while helping them to learn how to trust their conscience and have faith in God and themselves. Most of what our children learn is from our example. If your children are grown and you are feeling guilty for your mistakes, ask for forgiveness, and then let all that go and live as the wonderful person you are now.

Wholeness Generates Wholeness

A Delphic maxim tells us: "When you know yourselves, then you will be known, and you will understand that you are children of the living father. But if you do not know yourselves, then you dwell in poverty, and you are poverty."

Self-alienation is the root of our suffering and frustration in a relationship. Believing there is something wrong with us distorts our perception of our divine character. From this distortion springs aberrant mental and emotional states that result in cruel and pathetic behavior. Fanatically trying to be perfect and acceptable by the standards that others have set for us — so that we will be loved, adored, and taken care of — makes us neurotic, even psychotic, when it becomes too much for us to bear and our true self feels completely repressed. A sign of self-alienation is that, instead of expressing our innate beauty and divine characteristics by doing what we want and living in a way that supports our spiritual and creative evolution and development, we endeavor to become happy and prosperous by molding ourselves into someone we are not.

Adhering to artificial rules and regulations imposed on us by those who do not know that they and we are perfect children of God stifles our free self-expression. Then, instead of being in touch with our feelings, inner guidance system, and heartfelt desires, we allow the thoughts that are streaming from our subconscious mind and the minds of others to control our feelings and actions. Remember that you cannot trust your mind but you can trust yourself to know what is right and true for you and what isn't. By knowing who you are as a godlike being made in the image and likeness of the Supreme Being, the Creator, you are able to consciously direct your creative powers of manifestation to bring to you whatever you need and desire.

The Golden Rule Is Golden

Treat all others with respect and honor their freedom to be, do, and have what they choose as we also honor ourselves and our freedom to be, do, and have what we choose. Relationships are easy when we live by the Golden Rule and speak and behave toward others in the manner that we would like others to speak and behave toward us. In this way we do not need to memorize phrases and complicated theories in psychology but just think before we speak or act. Before speaking or acting, take a few moments and contemplate what you will say and how you will say it, as well as the other person's possible reactions to your words and actions. This can be practiced in the mind even before we have an encounter when we know how the other person usually reacts to us or how our previous behavior has produced a defensive reaction in the other. Make a memory, a new habit, by repeating the desired behavior in your imagination. In this way, we can train ourselves to think and act as we now choose instead of the way we did. We are always free to create a new habit and memory by doing the act over and over in our mind so that when the situation presents itself our first response is our new, chosen response. Also check your motive and intention behind your words and actions for it is the intention that will also be communicated. Remember that as you are intuitive and empathic, so are others. Most all communication is on the feeling and non-verbal level. Words are often used to lie and cover the truth, but we all know the truth for we feel it.

Be kind to all living entities, speak sweet words, and seek to be a beacon of inspiration, enthusiasm, and encouragement to all. Kindness and sweet words are always music to the ears and heart of anyone. Everyone loves words of adoration and appreciation. Showing affection, speaking sweetly, and paying attention to our loved ones express our love. Avoiding eye contact, using harsh words or sarcasm, embarrassing them in front of others, and constantly pointing out the flaws we perceive in them do not make for loving relationships. Before we speak, we should pause to think about our listener's feelings. No one likes to be attacked verbally or in any other way. It's far better to say, "I don't understand what you are saying" than "You don't make sense." "I feel embarrassed by what you said" is a more empowering statement than "You embarrassed me." There is no need to put someone on the defensive. This is the strategy of an abuser. You may hear people say things like: "What's the matter with you, can't you do anything right?" "The trouble with you is . . . ," "You'll never amount to anything," "No one likes you," "You will starve without me," "You make me sick," "You are killing your father," "You are a disappointment to me and others," or "You are ruining my life." This is emotional blackmail and the words of a person who will go to any lengths to hurt someone because she is hurting within. Every person is sovereign and responsible for herself, what happens to her, and her feelings, whether she wants to accept this or not. In some cases, one person's attachment to another is so strong that he will threaten to hurt himself in some way just to control the other person's behavior, as illustrated in the following story.

Once there were two friends who lived near each other and who felt rivalrous toward each other. One of the men grew tired of their bickering and decided to go on a long vacation and spiritual quest to get away and have some peace and quiet. The other man did not like this idea, since he enjoyed their bickering and the opportunity to harass his neighbor.

The antagonistic man thought about how he could stop his neighbor from leaving. He remembered that his neighbor was superstitious, so he read a book on superstitions. He found one that was perfect for his situation: "If, before a trip, you see someone whose nose has been amputated, this is a bad omen and you should immediately cancel your trip and stay home." This foolish and envious neighbor seized this opportunity and cut off the end of his own nose. Then he sat in front of the other man's house waiting for him to come out.

As the man came out of his house to begin his journey, he saw his friend with the amputated nose. Immediately, he remembered that this was a very bad omen, so he cancelled his vacation and went back inside. Some people will hurt themselves and be miserable just to ruin another person's joy.

We must always consider the source, the consciousness of the person speaking, and practice detachment and tolerance. There's no need to retaliate and strike back at others for their unkind remarks, or to feel hatred; doing so only makes us feel worse and guarantees that we will continue to engage in such a disempowering game. People play games like this only because they don't know how to behave in loving relationships and they mistake this kind of behavior and game playing as what relationships are about. This is what they see on television and in movies and also on the news. Some people believe that happy relationships are boring, but they are anything but boring. If we are bored it's because we are boring. It's important for each of us to be engaged in doing our life's work and developing our godlike nature through our spiritual practices or otherwise we can become obsessed by the relationship just because that is all we have going for us.

We are here to develop our godlike nature and to bloom into the fullness of our divine potential and greatness, not to squabble over things or to prove who is right and who is wrong. People who do this have the core belief that they are wrong and bad and feel so miserable that in order to be relieved of this they seek to make others wrong and bad. My mother always said, when my sisters and I were arguing: "It takes two to argue." If you do not come back with anger, or disagreement, there is no argument. Or think of a rope with a person on either end. As long as both are playing tug of war, there is a battle, but if either one drops the rope and walks off, the battle is over.

Be willing for others to be happy, prosperous, and successful in their endeavors and for us to be happy, prosperous, and successful in our endeavors.

Envy in any relationship interferes with how much intimacy each can attain and the degree to which the participants can cooperate and enjoy the benefits that two or more persons working in harmony are able to have. When envy raises its ugly head, there is competition. This can happen even in relationships with our closest friends and family members. The Old Testament story of Cain killing his brother, Abel, is a classic example of the dangers and foolishness of sibling rivalry. Preventing another from being happy, fortunate, or loved by others never gives envious people the real pleasure they seek, but deprives them of the flow of bliss that is waiting for them to soften and open their hearts and receive this gift from God. Bliss is unlimited and ever increasing when we drop our defenses that instead of protecting us from pain are creating pain. There is no greater pain than the restriction of the flow of love, for love is what we are.

Reciprocation

Ideal and lasting relationships are about reciprocating while in a giving mood. God is a giver, and we, as parts of God, and possessing the qualities of God, are also givers. When each of us exists for giving, for contributing, then even the act of receiving is an act of giving pleasure to the giver. Giving is a greater pleasure than receiving and yet unless we are willing to receive money, resources, and whatever we need, we will not be able to give as much as we would like. For example, if a singer does not sing, her talent lies dormant and so does her satisfaction and prosperity. But if the singer sings her song but is not willing to receive money and resources in exchange for sharing her talent, she may need to do other work in order to pay her bills.

Children who are allowed to give, to participate, to help out, to have chores, and who contribute in their spiritual community become successful, self-satisfied human beings. Givers are happy and prosperous, while the miserly are miserable and impoverished. Misers are always miserable. They believe that their miserable condition is always someone else's fault and never theirs. In a moment they could change this, simply by an act of giving, even if only a compliment or a helpful hand. When we do not allow our children to give to us and contribute to others, we are cheating them and condemning them to a life of unhappiness, for it is only the contributors, the givers, who experience self-worth, confidence, and satisfaction.

Purpose-Driven Relationships

There is a higher purpose for all of our relationships, and it is the same as the purpose for our businesses and us — God-consciousness. When our purpose is great enough, all our activities and relationships fit within it and work together to give us our highest and best benefits and advantages. There is no greater purpose than God-consciousness, for this gives us the topmost options of what is possible for anyone to attain. With God-consciousness we have the awareness of God. When we understand that there is a purpose for our being on earth, in these bodies, and in relationship, other than just to survive for a while and then die and lose everything we have worked for, including all our relationships,

possessions, and accomplishments, then we exist on the transcendental platform and our lives have meaning and direction.
Decisions are easier because we know what we want to accomplish and attain, and nothing we do is whimsical but contributes
to the attainment of our life's purpose.

Knowing our higher purpose is the saving grace in our relationships because each encounter with another person can be used
to develop our relationship skills and improve the quality of all
our other relationships now and in the future. I often tell my students, "Practice on the relationship you have instead of waiting
for the right person to show up." I say, "How will you know how
to treat Mr. or Ms. Right if you aren't treating people this way
now?" Because we are creatures of habit, we must develop the
habits of successful relating now in order to know how to relate
later on. Each encounter with another soul is an opportunity to
practice our godlike nature and thus improve the quality of all
our relationships.

Relationships are roles we play in God's drama called life.
Mother, father, child, husband, wife, boss, grandparent, sibling,
teacher, protector, spiritual teacher, doctor, and friend are roles.
But we are not the role we are playing any more than an actor in
a movie is the role they are playing. Roles have functions for the
overall success of the players and for the society in general, but
the roles are temporary and not eternal identities. With our children we play the role of parents until they reach a certain age, and
then we are their friends and only parents when needed to give
comfort and understanding. Playing the role of mother as we did
when our children were infants and dependent upon us does not
work when they are forty years old. Partners in marriage have
agreed-upon roles, and these are also in a stage of flux, for times

are changing. Teachers have a role that is distinct from the student, but later on the teacher may become the employee of this former student. What roles are you playing? Roles are like job descriptions or positions on a team, where each role is important for the overall success of the family, business, or sport. Remember, we have roles, we are not the roles. The problems come when we have preconceived notions about what our roles mean or we identify ourselves as the role. This is why partners in relationship need to discuss this topic and make their agreements, which can always change when necessary. Nothing is set in stone and all is flexible. When the role changes or is gone, there is an identity crisis unless the person realizes her eternal identity as a soul, the beloved of God.

Each person has a role to play in the success of the family, business, or organization, and when this is understood and each does his part, benefits for one and all are increased enormously. But if the participants work against the other members because of competition, hurt feelings, or resentment, good fortune stays far away. Remember that the Goddess of Fortune stays where there is harmony.

Forgiveness

Forgiveness is our salvation. It frees us from setting another unwanted karmic cycle in motion, and it releases us from unhappiness generated by the self-abuse of negative emotions such as resentment, anger, and hatred. Forgiveness releases the river of love and bliss and lets it flow through us so we experience the spiritual riches that everyone is trying to get. Until they understand that what they are seeking, they meet only frustration. Tolerance helps us to rise above the slings and arrows that may be coming from envious or angry people. This happens to celebrities and other public figures; people both adore and envy them. When our happiness is the result of others' adoration, we must remember that the mind is fickle and can change in a moment.

Once we understand the character and mind-set of people we know who tend to behave badly toward us, we need never be disappointed, carry a grudge, or use our precious energy to get even and pay them back. Why? Because we know these people will be true to their characters and conditioned natures. How can you expect kind and generous treatment from a person who believes in scarcity? When you serve a miser, you can never prosper and will always be disappointed. And if we forget that this is how such people have always behaved because of their fear- and lack-based conditioning, we will allow them to discourage or stop us from doing what we want or from being happy. Avoid people you know are unkind. If you must be around them, never fall to their level of consciousness. Use your time with them as a test. Pass the test by staying true to yourself at all times.

Forgiveness is about understanding that whatever we experience as our karmic schooling is the perfect way for us to learn a valuable lesson necessary for our soul evolution and expression. If we hate the person who delivers our karmic lesson or God, this does not free us but instead prolongs our suffering. If that person had not delivered the lesson, another would have been there to do so. Seeking revenge, we will only perpetuate our problems, because our actions will set a new karmic cycle of cause and effect in action.

We must never allow anyone or anything to take away our bliss. Let it flow regardless of what is happening, and continue to go forth to do your life's work and live as you choose. Envious people want us to stop and give up our life's work, as if this will give them more of whatever they believe we are taking from them by our success, happiness, and good fortune. Go forth with a peaceful mind and a happy heart and prosper regardless of how you are treated and regardless of what anyone says or does. This means keeping your eye focused on your path.

Begin Fresh in Every Moment

The best way to keep our love fresh and vital is to perceive others as souls, as perfect children of Mother/Father God. See their true, beautiful selves and not through a veil of all their mistakes and flaws, but as you saw and fell in love with them for the first time. Whatever is going on in a person's life, and how that person behaves, do not indicate who the person is, but instead is the result of her choices. We are not our choices. We are superior to whatever happens in the outer world, for we are the gods, the co-creators, and not the created. Material bodies are created, but we aren't. Our choices, unless we are enlightened, Self-realized, are the result of our programming — what we have been taught to believe is true and what we think we must do in order to be happy and prosperous.

If we want to stay in love, then we must perceive our loved ones fresh in each moment as their true, perfect selves. Think of every moment as a fresh moment, not as the extension of the moment before. Let it all go from your mind. Anything that was said or done in the past is over, unless we hold on to it and use it to spoil this moment and the next.

Carrying around a list of accumulated injustices, mistakes, hurtful words, and unfulfilled expectations performed by each of the people we know, in order to prove that they are bad and we are good, or that they are wrong and we are right, does not generate pleasure, so why do it? If there is no pleasure, what is the point? Living in the mind never brings supreme pleasure to our soul, only living from our heart does.

Excessive faultfinding is a sign that two partners are not getting what they wanted out of their relationship, and this shows that their intention was to get something, instead of to give. When they can no longer stand their thought-generated misery, the blaming goes into full swing. Anger and hatred emerge, and then the partners want to ruin each other — even though each was once head over heels in love with the other. But if the two really do have feelings for each other, then the key to restoring the relationship is to stop all criticisms, complaints, and blaming. Read this chapter a few times, make some agreements suggested in this chapter, and use the relationship to learn how to love someone unconditionally. Seek to be a pleasure giver and not a pleasure getter. The miracle happens when we find that by our selfless giving to our mate for his or her pleasure we actually receive the most pleasure.

But if we decide that it is not in our best interest spiritually to continue a relationship, there is never a need to be miserable by generating hate. Make the changes you feel guided to make without trying to destroy the other person as a way to punish him. We can continue to perceive his true, spiritual self while also understanding that we do not need to be in the relationship any longer as this is not the way we choose to live. Every person has the right to live as he or she chooses. We do not need to make someone else bad and wrong just because another wants to live in a way that is not our choice.

Giving Is the Source of the Greatest Sexual Pleasure

Sex has two purposes: first, it gives another soul, a child, the opportunity to incarnate into a loving family and become God-conscious and live forever in bliss. The other purpose is soul-to-soul lovemaking, a way to be as intimate, loving, and vulnerable as possible, to express the fullness of our loving feelings of affection and give pleasure to the person who is the object of our affection. Because sex is such a powerful uniting of body fluids and the union between a soul and matter at the moment of conception, the mood and consciousness of the love-makers and parents-to-be are most important. This is why it is best for the parents to have healthy bodies, peaceful minds, and love for each other. Mating during a time of happiness, even in prayer, provides a divine space for an advanced soul to be conceived and birthed into this world. Like attracts like. Souls incarnate in bodies through parents that match their frequency signatures.

When we realize that our parents perfectly matched our consciousness, desires, karma, and God's will, how could we ever complain again? Complaining in this way would be cursing God, who is only trying to help us to develop our godlike nature through our karmic reactions as we live out our dreams in the material world. To better understand this process of karma, we need to know something about reincarnation, which I explain in the next chapter.

The real pleasure in sex, which includes but is also more than the physical release, is experienced when we learn the art of giving for our mate's pleasure without expecting to be pleasured. As strange as this seems, this is how it works. I know, because I'm an expert. My most pleasurable sex happened while I was married to a man who prematurely ejaculated. I didn't want to hurt his tender feelings, so I never mentioned that I wasn't getting pleasure in the way he thought, and I didn't even care about it. I'd already had many orgasms, so I didn't care about having more. I wanted a deeper, more satisfying soul experience. The pleasure I felt during our most intimate times was the most satisfying spiritually and physically that I've ever had, because my purpose was to let him experience pleasure and satisfaction. My worst times were when I expected my mate to pleasure me.

Maximum satisfaction and intimacy happens spontaneously when both partners give for the pleasure of the other, for now there is no difference between the lover and beloved, as they are one. The wedding ring is a symbol of unconditional, reciprocal love with no beginning or end, for this is the purpose of marriage — a commitment to God and yourself as well as your mate to use the marriage to fulfill your higher purpose by learning how to love another as yourself. Once we can do this with one person, we can also expand our sphere of unconditional love to include all others.

Generally speaking, people get into relationships to get something out of them, to use the other person for pleasure, money, and security. When this does not happen as planned, they seek other partners who will give them the pleasure and whatever else they seek. But the same frustrating situation happens again with each new partner. Selfless giving is free of the thought "What am I getting out of this?," because the giver is very happy and satisfied by the act of giving. Remember that giving and receiving are two sides of the same coin. Reciprocation is the way of mutually supportive and empowering relationships. But when one partner is consistently the giver and the other is the taker, the giver's feelings of love get stronger and the taker becomes exceedingly more demanding and angry because he is not experiencing happiness. No wonder!

How can we experience happiness when we expect others to make us happy? This is illustrated by the story of the foolish boy who wanted his parents to bring the moon and stars down from the sky so he could have them for his own. Because his parents couldn't do it, he jumped up and down with fury and screamed at his parents. Then the boy spit into the sky at God for not giving him what he wanted. The spit fell back down onto his face, for what we give out comes back to us — this is karma in action.

When we are full-time takers, self-consumed, treating others as objects and not persons with feelings, our personalities become confused. In time, takers come to hate the givers and, to justify their lack of reciprocation, must find faults in the giver. Although God is the owner and giver of everything, how many people find fault in God, blaming God for all the sorrows and troubles that we humans bring on ourselves? No matter how much takers get, it is never enough, and they attribute their misery to others, including God. The unhappy taker becomes more and more demanding and more and more abusive, punishing others for his pain and lack. The giver has already experienced full satisfaction from the joy of giving. When we perceive life through material vision, the filter of our conditioning, we believe in lack; conversely, by perceiving everyone and everything through spiritual vision, we find that abundance is all there is.

Practicing Heaven on Earth

Families are either the training ground for insanity or for the bliss, health, and good fortune of their members. No one wants to believe that she is bad and a disappointment to the very people she wants to please. Stern, disapproving looks, sarcastic words, public humiliation, and threats of violence all impede the evolution of the soul.

A seed planted in the soil cannot grow when repeatedly stomped on — it will shrivel and die. Souls blossom in a healthy environment in which each person is respected and appreciated and perceived as a perfect child of God instead of a collection of molecules that make up the physical body.

Resolve now to stop criticizing anyone, including your children, as this is a painful and manipulative device that will only backfire on you in time. It encourages others to shut down, lie to you, and find other ways to be happy that don't include you. God doesn't criticize us, but loves and adores us forever and ever. Our work is to treat others with mercy and compassion, as God treats us. Jesus told his disciples: "A new commandment I give unto you, That ye love one another; as I have loved you, that ye also love one another" (John 13:34). This scripture doesn't mention retribution, an eye for an eye. Jesus came from the spiritual world to give us a glimpse into our superior, spiritual home and to tell us about who we really are and what is possible for each of us to attain: a beautiful, sweet, and opulent life forever. Earth is our training ground, where we are practicing for our eternal future. Whatever we are doing now is creating what will happen in the future. This is manifesting 101, the basic teaching of metaphysics.

Revealing Perfection

Once a sculptor was asked how he could make a statue of a woman from a large granite stone. He replied, "I just chisel away what is not needed, so that the form of a woman's body, already existing as a potential in the stone, is revealed."

We are already perfect; our work is to let go of what has nothing to do with us, including all the rules, regulations, false concepts, and fear-based beliefs that our subconscious minds have been programmed with so that we can be controlled, dominated, and manipulated to do the will of others instead of following our own inner guidance and spiritual path. We must be spiritually intelligent and courageous if we choose to take back our soul power and fulfill our divine destiny. As long as we are afraid, we are never free.

As it states in the Bhagavad Gita: "Being freed from attachment, fear and anger, being fully absorbed in God and taking refuge in God, many, many persons in the past became purified by knowledge of God — and thus they all attained transcendental love for God" (4.10).

A God-conscious person is fearless, for she has surrendered to the will of Mother/Father God and so lives in peace, detached from this world and everyone and everything within it, which are all temporary anyway. We will lose everything material: all prestige, money, and fame when we leave these bodies for other bodies. Detachment does not mean we do not care about others or what happens — not at all. Detachment means we know how life works. We realize that, although we love others with all our hearts and wish them well, we know that all souls, including our sweet animal friends, are on their own paths of self-evolution and do not belong to us. Nor is it for us to interfere with their paths by using emotional blackmail, control, or abuse to make them conform to our plans for them. This is real love — the desire for our loved ones to be all they are capable of becoming. Kindness and compassion are the symptoms of a happy person.

Giving Up Meanness

Recognize that the way we are treating others is the way we are treating ourselves because what we give out is what we will get back. Cruelty to others, including animals and the earth, is a symptom of an unhappy person hurting from self-alienation because somewhere in her past she was abused, ridiculed, and subjected to pain when she was too small or weak to protect herself or get away. Notice how many cartoons, video games, and movies are about killing, maiming, or forcing people into submission, as if such actions are a game and something to enjoy. Mistreating others, including animals and the earth, is indefensible and a symptom of violence programming. Sooner or later, everything we have wished to happen to others, and what we have done to others, will happen to us, for this is how the immutable law of karma, the great leveler, works. If you catch yourself laughing at someone's misfortune, stop and ask yourself, "What is this about?" Having fun at the expense of others will backfire. A story about an elephant and a shopkeeper demonstrates this.

Once there was a man who had a shop in a village where he sold fruits and flowers. Every day a friendly, tame elephant would stop at the shop on his way to the river to take a bath. The shopkeeper would give the elephant a nice piece of fruit. In this way their friendship grew. However, one day the shopkeeper decided to play a joke on the elephant. Instead of giving him a piece of fruit, he pricked the elephant's trunk with a sharp pin. This made the elephant jump and run away in pain. A few heartless bystanders and the shopkeeper had a big laugh. This was not funny to the elephant. At the river after his bath, the elephant loaded his trunk with muddy water, walked back to the fruit and flower stand, and poured the muddy water over everything in the shop, ruining the shopkeeper's sales for the day. Feeling ashamed for what he had done, the shopkeeper tried to make amends, but the elephant never visited his shop again.

The Value of Momentary Shame

Although shame is not something we need to carry with us and indulge in, some shame is valuable. Momentary shame is a healthy emotion, and people who are able to feel shame are either awake, or awakening, to their spiritual nature. While it is true that others' emotions and reactions belong to them and are their responsibility, we cannot be cruel or cause anyone distress on purpose. Thinking that, since others' reactions are their problem, we can be as mean and insulting as possible causes us to fall into deeper levels of ignorance, creating more bad karma for us. Cruelty always comes back to the person who has been cruel, in the same way that love comes back to the one who treats others with love and affection. Spiritual people — you and I — are naturally compassionate, for we know how others feel, because we too have felt this way and know how important it is to be offered comfort, understanding, and encouragement. Karma is about reaping the favorable or unfavorable results of our actions. What we call unfavorable or bad karma is about feeling what another felt because of our actions born of envy or anger.

The moment we realize we have caused another distress because of an unkind remark, a misguided unkind action, or anything that we have done to hurt someone on purpose, it's best to understand the mistake, ask forgiveness, and make amends as quickly as possible. Then let it go and move on. Mentally going over and over the same situation for longer than a minute is not necessary. Correct yourself with positive reinforcement and help others to do the same. Each encounter with another person is an opportunity to build positive and life-affirming habits.

Keep the Best and Dump the Rest

Avoid the company of chronic criticizers, naysayers, prophets of doom, materialists, fearmongers, gossipers, and the fearful, envious, and angry. If you must be around these lower-frequency energies, consider it a test of your ability to hold your own and keep your mind, emotions, and words in the spiritual zone. When you can do this, you become victorious, not a victim. We must control our thoughts and words, or we are nothing more than stimulus-response machines reacting from habit and fear- and lack-based programming. Seek the highest truth and act on it, regardless of your old habits and programming. Remember that you are making new habits and these are what will now start manifesting.

No one can control you through your mind and emotions when you are controlling your mind and emotions and directing them as you choose. Never give this power away to anyone, ever. Challenge every belief, every bit of programming, and determine whether it is spiritually correct or a lie concocted by someone for the purpose of controlling you and others to do their perhaps nefarious will. Use your vote, your soul power, to manifest your heart's desires.

No one is required to stay in a situation that has become oppressive or is otherwise no longer suitable. This doesn't mean we should leave at the first sign of a problem, however. There are valuable lessons to be learned by developing our relationship skills — for what else is there other than our eternal relationship with our God and others? Before we run away, only to face the same situation again with others until we learn the lesson, it's a good idea to practice unconditional love on the people we are with. Practice makes perfect.

I have found that the key of transformation through relationships is to perceive each person that we interact with, especially the ones we are in closest contact with, as a mirror reflection of ourselves. In this way, rather than being angry at or disappointed by their behavior, we understand that we have treated people the same way in the past, or that there is an opportunity to offer unconditional love, which works as a medicine to cure the disease of envy, by genuinely wishing them well. You will know in your heart whether it is time to go or time to stay in a relationship with someone, so trust your conscience. We know when a person is a blessing or a curse by whether we feel enlivened and happy in his presence or suppressed, discouraged, or harassed.

Remember that each encounter with another soul is an opportunity to practice unconditional love, which is exactly what we need in order to release ourselves from judging others as good and bad. This allows us to elevate our consciousness to the spiritual zone, where we are able to perceive the divine nature of all souls. And this liberates us from the lower-frequency realms of hell, where people are hating, competing, faultfinding, blaming, arguing, and fighting for survival by defeating others, who are Mother/Father God's precious children.

Our challenge is to stay blissful by flowing love to others, by expressing God's love through our feelings, and by holding our minds steady and peaceful in the transcendental realm. In spiritually motivated relationships, there is mutual cooperation, kindness, and empowerment; these relationships are made in heaven. The choice of heaven or hell is ours in this moment. This is the whole purpose of life. Don't worry if you forget and fall back into an old hellish habit — you will keep getting another chance until you get it right.

Happiness and Prosperity Practices

A. Observe why you like being with some people more than others. Observe the various roles you are playing in relationships. Observe whose rules and beliefs you have been following and why. Observe the way you talk to people, how you treat them, and the motive behind your words and treatment.

B. Contemplate each person you know. See him or her as a perfect soul who has the right to live as he or she chooses. Contemplate the lessons that have come to you in your personal and business relationships. Use the following declarations: Today, I refuse to judge or criticize anyone. Today, I choose to associate with kind, generous, and honest people. Today, I make my relationship decisions based on people's behavior and not their promises. Today, I will treat others with love, and I will respect their right to do what they want and live as they choose.

C. Act as if you are as you desire to be, and you will be: before you speak or behave, pause, take a few breaths, and sense what your conscience, and not your programmed mind, is telling you. Behave in the way that you want people to behave toward you, and which is consistent with your spiritual nature and life's purpose.

Prospering Mantras

My perfect mate is now manifesting in my life.
I have the right to choose relationships that are mutually enriching.
I perceive each person as a child of God and my eternal family member.
I am grateful for all my relationships that have taught, and are teaching, me to love unconditionally.

CHAPTER SIX

*Who Were You Before,
and Who Will You Be Next?*

We always get another chance to attain the goal of our lives — the supreme and eternal pleasure of our soul. The principle of endless chances is called reincarnation. Reincarnation means rebirth, to be born again, after death, in a new body to a new set of parents in a new set of circumstances in order to continue with our lessons, manifest our desires, and attain what we started but did not complete in the previous incarnation. Think of a child prodigy who at four years of age is able to play the piano much better than a trained middle-aged pianist. The child had to have been an expert in his previous lifetime.

Human life is conscious mentality encased in flesh, but it is not the flesh. Knowing ourselves as mere physical bodies is the densest level of consciousness, for in that case the soul is weighted down by the heaviness of material energy instead of being the operator of this material energy. Soul bodies are never born, so we can never die. These temporary physical bodies, however, which are made of flesh, bones, muscles, and such, have a beginning, continue for a while, and then end when the body is no longer a suitable vehicle for the soul. But the soul lives on, seeking a new form to express itself through.

Reincarnation explains why one child is born into a wealthy family and another into the most wretched and impoverished situation. It may appear that God is kind to some and is harsh to others, but this is not the case. People who do not understand or accept reincarnation must then accept that God is not fair and gives some plenty of food and others nothing, letting them starve. This type of God, who causes people to suffer, cannot be a loving and good God. No one gets only one chance to attain God-consciousness, the complete liberation from all miseries. It is a gradual process of awakening from the darkness of ignorance into full enlightenment, into Self-realization. Enlightenment brings the end of suffering, for the enlightened person discovers who she is and has the knowledge to successfully navigate the waters of material life and live as she chooses.

By absorbing our minds in the most spiritually elevated and beautiful thoughts possible, we will attain what these thoughts point to. Similarly, if we focus on hideous thoughts, we will then obtain the results of those thoughts. The process we are using now to get what we want — developing our consciousness by means of what we learn and do — works exactly the same way as reincarnation: it is a process of action and reaction. A life of worldly joy and comfort is the result of good karma; a life of sorrow and hardship is the result of bad karma. But our saving grace is that even what is called bad karma can be a blessing when we use it to learn — when we drop all previous fear- and lack-based programming and go forth as our true, divine selves on a mission of love. God gives all that he has to his children when they want to have it.

When one chapter of our life in the material realm ends, the next chapter begins where we left off. Loss of the body does not turn an angry person into a happy person, just as changing our clothes does not change our conditioned nature; this we must do by upgrading our consciousness. All material forms and events in our lives were originally thoughts and desires in either God's mind or ours. In science, torsion physics explains how consciousness translates into matter and events on the earth and throughout the physical universe. Consciousness creates and changes material energy. At the highest soul level, there is no reincarnation — no different lives — only one continuous life in which we simply transmigrate from one form and set of circumstances to the next. There is a purpose behind the manifested realms, and it is for us to realize and express our eternal godlike nature and take our rightful place in the grand scheme as fully realized and actualized gods and goddesses whose only purpose and consciousness is love and bliss. Remember that you and I are the bliss of the universe; this is our only work, our only function, and our only purpose. Realizing this can take billions and billions of universe years or just one lifetime — the choice is ours.

Discussion of reincarnation was excluded from the Holy Bible as a way to keep people in ignorance about who they are as spiritual beings, equal to all other souls. It was also a way to keep them terrified of eternal hell, which was said to be their punishment by a wrathful God if they broke the rules set by the leaders of their religion. Then, to reinforce their fear, people were told that to even question what was being taught would mean expulsion from the church, possible torture in prison, confiscation of their properties, and eternal damnation and suffering. None of this is true about God but is the work of people desiring to manipulate the believers.

The God I know and serve with love and devotion is kind, loving, and sweet. The Supreme Being never judges or condemns anyone to an eternity of hellish tortures, but protects and adores each and every one of us now and always, in the same way that a loving mother protects and showers her babies with love. However, because we are in the school of material energy that surrounds each soul in the form of the subtle body — made of mind and false ego — and the gross physical body, we are subject to the laws of karma: action and reaction.

The beginning step of God-consciousness is the realization that our identity is not the material body that is born, creates some products and services, and then dies. Instead our identity is purely spiritual. Souls encased in subtle bodies transmigrate from one material body to the next, one situation to the next, for the higher purpose of ultimately attaining liberation from this realm, if we choose to do so, and reaching the spiritual realms inhabited by superior beings who are never born and never die, but live eternally in bliss, beauty, and opulence. It's true that there is only one life: one continuous life with no beginning or end. We recognize this when we understand the indestructible nature of each and every soul. One chapter ends as the next one begins. In reincarnation, we always get another chance to attain whatever we desire materially or spiritually through the process of taking on the consciousness that will manifest what we desire. Remember: "act as if you are as you desire to be, and you will be" is the secret for attaining whatever appeals to us.

Reincarnation is the process by which souls stuck in old and sick bodies can start fresh and get another chance to live out their dreams and make spiritual progress, but it is also a continual process that happens on a daily basis when we discard an unwanted attitude or way of being for a new and improved one. I have had many lifetimes while in this current so-called lifetime, and so have you. Every time we reinvent ourselves by making a major change in consciousness, career, and lifestyle, we leave the old behind as we take up the new, but we continue to exist throughout these changes. Cells die off and new cells are created, our hair is cut and new hair grows, and we move from one house to another and one friend to another in the same way that seasons change. We witness it all but transcend the whole process.

Many Past Lives

My study of reincarnation started when I was in high school. Being concerned about dying, I was drawn to information about past lives. One day while hunting through the shelves at the school library, looking for something that interested me enough to read it, I came across some books on reincarnation. This subject fascinated me, but it wasn't taught in any of the churches I visited or in school, or talked about by anyone I knew except my great-grandmother. While I knew that we all lose our bodies at some point, the idea of being dead seemed too awful to even think about. But of course I had to think about it. I had lost a couple of grandparents already — they had been alive one moment and gone the next. My great-grandmother had been a nurse and had told me about seeing a blue light leave people's bodies at the moment they died, or shall we say left their bodies.

Reincarnation was the subject that started me on my spiritual quest. Who am I, where did I come from, what am I supposed to be doing while I am here, and where am I going after I leave my current body? I wanted to know the answers to these questions, and although no one else that I knew in high school even thought about these things, I felt guided to find out. But I kept my quest to myself for fear of being ridiculed or thought of as weird, a devil, or a heretic. It's amazing how truth is suppressed simply by our fear of what others will think of us and what they and God will do to us for being curious and exploring outside the boundaries of what we have been conditioned to believe is true. God never punishes anyone, and he understands our curious nature, for we got this nature from our Source.

Since that time, many of my past lives have been revealed to me through various spiritual therapies and practices. There is no way to prove that any of them were my lives, but my visions and feelings have told me they were. Our greatest challenge in self-discovery is to trust our own experiences instead of other people who deny our experiences. In each of my past-life recollections, I saw a vivid scene, including a location, people, and events. Each lifetime that was revealed to me contained a lesson and sometimes a traumatic experience that I had formulated into a belief that was still manifesting itself in my present incarnation. The reason we are able to recall previous bodies and lifetimes is that memories of them are contained within the memory bank of the subconscious, the subtle body, which travels with us and surrounds us as we take on new bodies, lifetime after lifetime.

Recalling past lives is important therapy; it helped me to understand some issues I was dealing with and why they were presenting themselves in my present incarnation. Understanding the process of reincarnation and recalling any of your past life experiences gives you the direct experience that you do not die, that you live forever. Bodies change, but souls continue. The Bhagavad Gita tells us: "For the soul there is neither birth nor death at any time. He has not come into being, does not come into being, and will not come into being. He is unborn, eternal, ever-existing, and primeval. He is not slain when the body is slain" (2.20).

Ascension to the Higher Realms

The greatest fear is the fear of death, and this fear lurks within our minds as we contemplate when and how we will leave our present bodies. Some people are so attached to their bodies, houses, relationships, and things that, even after these people are taken from their bodies, they continue to hover around all that they are attached to. They are not seen, except by the people who have extrasensory perception, nor can they get any pleasure from their senses.

When it is time to go on, it is wise for us to detach ourselves from the physical plane and cling to the spiritual, to God who is with us, and lift off into the higher realms of soul pleasures. This place is not all that exists; it is a training center where souls can learn to awaken to the point that their consciousness is pure enough to be in the company of other souls who live in the realms of unconditional love and opulence. Just as there are levels of accomplishment and expertise in mundane activities and grades in school, such as third and fourth grades, there are also unlimited numbers of realms and planes of existence in the material and spiritual worlds that are attained when one becomes qualified to do so. Qualification is determined by consciousness — by how we treat others and what we are doing with our resources, minds, and bodies.

Fear of death is so strong in some people that they never really live. Fear does not prevent us from leaving our bodies when it is our time. The sacred literature mentions cases where people have taken their bodies with them. But this can happen only when a person's love of God is so strong that his body is transfigured. Ancient Hebrew, Vedic, and Sumerian writings testify to people being taken up by spacecraft. Whatever happens, life is not about the body, but about us becoming God-conscious, pure love and bliss. When this happens, we are free to be wherever we choose.

Although the physical body is important for our spiritual education, it is not who we are or all that is possible for us to attain. Without higher knowledge, people think about and desire only what they have thought about and desired. This is all they can experience until they open their minds and receive information way beyond what they have known or what has been taught in formal government-created and religious educational systems. Of what value is the gift of human life if not used fully or if it is lived in a tiny box, when there are universes of possibilities available to us all, simply for the asking?

Cowards die from fear in every moment. The courageous never die; they ascend, leaving behind what is no longer needed or doesn't resonate at their higher-frequency signatures. We are here to live our dreams and practice being our true selves while in a physical body; this is how the training works. God, as the Supersoul, resides with each of us in the temple of the heart, the temple of the body, guiding us — we need to tune in and receive the communication. There is a purpose to life and death, which is attained when we live an abundant life. The Bible tells us: "I am come that they might have life, and that they might have [it] more abundantly" (John 10:10). Abundant life means that we allow our spirit, our talents, and our divine nature to express themselves fully, free of repressive and limiting subconscious programming. It means being fully alive instead of hiding from death or the criticisms and ridicule of the unenlightened.

Where Do All These Souls Come From?

Some may wonder: "If there are more people now than ever before, where did these new souls come from?" Eastern mysticism tells us that living entities, souls, occupy the bodies of all creatures, that there are 8,400,000 different species of life and an unlimited number of living entities in billions of universes and occupying the forms of these various species. Vedic knowledge tells us that souls evolve from the simplest organism up to the human, the most exalted of all. The human mind and body are designed to enable the full awakening of the soul into cosmic and God-consciousness; all godly qualities manifest through that soul forever. Consciousness is the determining factor for the existence of a soul.

Humanity is superior to other species from the standpoint of our divine intelligence and position as a caretaker of the other species, but this is not for the purpose of committing violence on others. Violence is justified by the ignorant who seek to own, control, abuse, and kill the creatures deemed soulless and without rights and consciousness, which includes feelings. We can witness the results of this concept.

Animals Have Souls

Any physical body that moves, including that of any insect, must have a living entity, a soul, within it operating it along with the Supersoul, unless it is the mechanical, computerized, or biotechnological creation of some mad scientist. Souls are atomic in size, and because they are not made of material energy, they are superior to, and not subject to, the laws of nature as the physical body and the inanimate world are. How could any form of inert matter move unless there was someone moving it, operating it? We can see that, once a soul leaves, the eyes, ears, digestion, mouth, heart, organs, arms, and legs fall limp and become vacant, just as a house that was occupied becomes vacant when the former tenant leaves.

Anyone with a pet knows that animals have personalities and feelings. Why else would dogs be called "man's best friend"? I have spent many wonderful hours taking care of cows and have been privileged to witness their sweetness and their love for their babies and cow friends. Once we recognize that all living creatures are souls engaged in evolving from unconsciousness to consciousness, we can have loving relations with everyone and all creatures great and small. The souls within all bodies are equal and sentient, and they are the children of God at various levels of soul evolution. However, human beings have special powers, given our position as caretakers of the creation because of our level of intelligence and our capabilities. All creatures have a right to live out their lives peacefully, so that they can continue up the ladder of soul evolution.

A human body is the most prized, for it gives us the opportunity and capability to learn about who we are as spiritual beings, to learn about our relationship with God, and to activate all our godly qualities, including intelligence, healing, telepathy, and cosmic abilities. Through the mystic powers of the Divine Mind, we can travel interdimensionally. Any human being can take the next giant step in soul evolution — to Self-realization and actualization. But there are stories of amazing animals that have performed great acts of devotion and love. Some of these souls in animal bodies apparently had full awareness of who they were as souls, but had a function to perform and a lesson to learn in their animal bodies.

Perceiving the Spiritual

Once we attain Self-realization, our original spiritual body — including the mind and senses — is awakened and becomes fully operational. Some search the sky for answers, adventure, and amazing experiences, and some seek to find their roots and treasures in the inner realm, the source and prototype of all outer worlds. Inner vision permits entrance into the higher realm beyond the spheres of matter and beyond the scope of any mechanical technology or human laws, through the portal of the soul.

This purely spiritual universe, available only to souls who are free of the gross limitations of material energy, has a Sanskrit name, Vaikunta, meaning "free of anxiety." It is a place of limitless bliss, beauty, and every conceivable form of wealth, and can be attained while in the material body temple by souls who know who they are. They no longer identify the body as the self, but identify God as their Self and the Self of every soul. God's will before creation was: "I am One, and I wish to be the Many." God expanded to become the many, and we constitute that expansion. God is one, but willed himself to become many for his enjoyment, so we exist for his pleasure. His creation is the manifestation of his will's motion toward variety, for variety is the spice of life.

Material universes are places where birth, death, old age, disease, and death abide. Spiritual universes are devoid of these and are opulent, eternal, and purely blissful in every way. Some may find this a challenge to contemplate because they are influenced by the dense and dark material energy that envelopes the soul like a shroud and blocks their ability to know what is beyond this shroud of darkness. Such people accept that life is getting worse as they live in fear of future misfortune and suffering, and they close their minds to a reality that is superior to this one and full of opulence that they can live in now, in their consciousness. The Lord's prayer, given to us by Jesus, states, "as in Heaven so on Earth." This tells us we can manifest the spiritual domain on earth, and in fact this is what we are supposed to be doing.

Whatever our desire, our greatest obstacle is our programming. Believing only in what we can sense with our material senses limits us to what we have known, been taught, or experienced. Perceiving the spiritual takes spiritual senses. Our souls are pure spirit. We must trust our feelings, not our material minds, past experiences, or only what we have been taught to believe is true.

We've Been It All

During our travels in the material realm, we have been kings, queens, beggars, thieves, leaders, followers, extraterrestrials, and nobodies. We've been rich, poor, beautiful, ugly, cruel, and good. Truly we human beings are one family, whatever our religion, color, nationality, or role. This is why identifying ourselves as our bodies — or identifying with a religion, sex, nationality, social position, or financial condition, or anything related to the body, or thinking in terms of "us versus them," or being prejudiced and hating someone because of his appearance or beliefs — is the ultimate of ignorance and foolishness. The body we get is the one we earned through karma and our desires; it was deemed the perfect vehicle for us to learn our lessons and develop our divine nature of love and super intelligence.

Victimizers today will be victimized in the future in exactly the same way they treated others. Leaders who work to cheat their people will be among the cheated and abused in their next lives. The most pious persons will earn lofty positions of wealth and power in their next lives, but will still lose it all in the one after, unless they use their wealth in service to God for the good of all. Everything belongs to God and is to be used in God's service. We advance by our pious deeds, which return only good fortune.

Bodies recycle into new bodies for souls to continue to live their dreams while harvesting the crop of results sown by their previous actions. Whatever we have done or caused to happen follows us as surely as the day follows the night. Some people think that, for example, pollution is not their problem, because they will be gone from here one day. But they will be back and will experience its effects, or be born on another planet where they will have the opportunity to reap what they have sown.

Everyone is creating his next body and future conditions by what he is thinking, desiring, feeling, imagining, and doing now. The subtle body, which is made up of the mind and false ego, and which surrounds the soul, contains all the information about every lifetime we've experienced, including all the details of our present incarnation. What we call a past life was just us in a different body, with a different name, family, career, and so on.

Near Death

Reading about near-death experiences can help us remember that we are not the roles we are playing or the bodies we occupy; however, bodies are very important — they are the greatest treasure in this world — or we wouldn't have them. Committing suicide is never a good idea, because the person who commits suicide does not solve his problems or end his suffering with the destruction of the body. In his next life, he will take up where his past life left off, and he will have to meet the exact same problems again. The test of unconditional love will arrive again, and will continue to do so until the test has been passed. After committing suicide, a person has to hover in the plane of discarnate beings until the appointed time for his natural departure, and this is not pleasant. It's best to learn how to flow love and bliss regardless of what is happening or how we are treated by others. Then we can always be happy, instead of making others responsible for our feelings and prosperity.

We have each had experiences where we feel strongly attracted or repelled by someone, which usually means we have known this person in a past life. People who have great love for each other will reincarnate many times together, and groups of souls may also incarnate together for a common purpose.

We Are Creating Our Next Life Now

Transmigration of the soul takes place in this lifetime as we progress from the body of a baby to that of a child, teenager, young adult, mature adult, and senior. While we are in our present bodies, new bodies, new parents, and new conditions are being prepared for us that are a perfect match for us, given our consciousness, karma, and desires, so that when our present bodies can no longer serve us on our journey and adventure, we can continue on with fresh garments. On this subject the Bhagavad Gita explains: "As a person puts on new garments, giving up the old ones, similarly, the soul accepts new material bodies giving up the old and useless ones" (1.22).

Have you ever thought about your next life and what you desire to be, do, and have? Because we do have a next life, or rather the continuation of our eternal life, we can choose what we want to be, do, and have in our next incarnation by the same process we use to manifest whatever we choose in this incarnation. The laws of nature and life do not change. You do have something to say about where you are going, what your life will be like, and what kind of body you will have. Some people think life will be over for them when they lose the body they have now, as if they are that body. But that's like saying your life is over when you trade in your old car for a new one. The Bhagavad Gita puts it this way: "Whatever state of being one remembers when he quits his body... that state he will attain without fail" (8.6). Our current lifetime is the result of what we did in our past lifetime, and so it goes.

It's a good idea to contemplate this topic. You do have a future lifetime, and it is being created now: as you sow, so shall you reap. When you know where you want to go and what you want your eternal life to be about, then you must start cocreating it now by planting seeds in the form of the desires, thoughts, words, and deeds that you hope will take root and manifest in your future. Some people take more time to plan a two-week vacation than their current lives or their next ones. What kind of a person do you want to be? What would you like to be doing? Where would you like to live? How do you want to spend your eternal life?

Nothing happens by accident or for no reason at all. To understand the process, I sought the highest knowledge possible, which explained about all the realms and possibilities that we can attain in the worlds of matter and the spiritual world. I am a serious pleasure seeker, so I sought knowledge offered by the most elevated and blissful souls, who possess the fullness of all mystic powers. There is a reading list at the end of the book if you are interested in doing your own research. Because this has been explained by much more evolved souls than myself, I suggest that you read their works and make your decisions.

There was a time when I wanted to be a temperamental opera singer in my next life. After my current body turned fifty, I thought, "Why wait for my next life; why not become an opera singer now?"

After deciding I would pursue this, I did my manifestation work and the perfect teacher, the maestro David Kyle, appeared in my life. He trained my voice and consciousness with exercises that I practiced over and over. Never criticizing me, he used positive and loving reinforcement, alerting me to the times when what I did was perfect. Yes, I became an opera singer. But I didn't like opera, except for Puccini arias. Then and there I realized that I did not want to make opera my career, now or in my next life. How relieved I was to know that I hadn't waited until my next life to find this out. I am so glad that I didn't wait and instead started doing now what I thought I wanted to do in the future. This is actually how it works — whatever you want to do in the future, begin it now. Otherwise, how can it happen in the future?

Whatever talent we want to develop, we will develop by taking instruction and practicing it. Genius is often developed over lifetimes. We are amazed at others' extraordinary capabilities, but when understood in light of reincarnation and the continuation of life, possessing such great abilities makes sense. One lifetime runs into the next because we are the same soul throughout all our lifetimes. The subtle mind holds these memories, and when we lay down one body for another we still experience continuity of consciousness.

The Best Way to Prepare to Leave

Death is not a bad experience to be feared. It's a cleansing experience, a chance to continue on in a new body with the new relatives and conditions that we have attracted by the law of karma. Perhaps you will be born as your own grandchild or great-grandchild so you can continue in the same family. More than this, death is a mystical portal, a star gate, an opportunity for us to enter into the eternal realms of beauty and pleasure beyond anything we have known or experienced before. Everyone will make this passage, as we have done countless times before. But very few ever think of death as a portal and an opportunity to get off the wheel of birth and death and enter the spiritual realms of eternal soul pleasures.

The predominant thought at the moment of death decides the next destination of the human soul. This thought is the culmination of a person's lifetime of activities, thoughts, attractions, interests, and desires. At this moment, between one lifetime experience and the next, God appears and asks us what we want. I practice what I will ask for and use my time in preparation for my next life by living the way I want to be in the future, now. What will you ask God for when it's your turn?

If you knew that God would appear to you and give you anything you asked for at the moment of your passing, what would you ask for? Consider the following fable. An old woman carrying a heavy load dropped it by the side of the road. Sitting down, she felt overwhelmed by despair and fatigue, so she prayed to God to help her. God appeared and asked her to tell him what she wanted him to do. "Lift the load back up on my head so that I may go home." The Lord did as she asked and then left. The old woman, who could have asked for anything, wasted her request, her vote, on something so ordinary and mundane that anyone could have done it. Be prepared to ask God for what you really want when you get the opportunity. You can do this now, for the presence of God is with you now and always. Thinking and asking big is a sign of greatness.

Where Is Your Attention?

Every moment is preparation for the next moment, and this includes the moment we spend between the two realms, spiritual and physical, at our appointed time of departure. Wherever we focus our attention is where we are going, and what we will manifest there depends on how we are using our free will at the time of departure. Thinking of the form of God we like, the form that gives us the greatest pleasure, takes us to our God. By remembering Jesus, we will go to the realm of Jesus. If we are thinking of Krishna and his lady love, Radha, we will go to the spiritual world of Vaikunta, their pleasure groves of divine love and play. Gandhi, with his last breath, spoke the name of Lord Rama, and so the realm of Lord Rama was his destination. Jesus at the moment of passing said first: "Forgive them Father, for they know not what they do"; and then he said, "O, Father, into thy hands I commit my spirit." Jesus went to his Father's kingdom, the kingdom of God.

If we are angry and full of hate at the time of the transition, we will go where this hatred takes us, where hate is the predominant emotion. Harboring resentment and anger toward God and whomever else you haven't forgiven will give you another round of troubles in your next lifetime. And deep affection for certain people will surely bring you and them together again. When we become soft-hearted, kind, and generous, then naturally others will treat us the same way in our next incarnation, for what we give out always returns to us. Life is not a game of chance; it is exact, and it works according to the laws of nature created and controlled by the Supreme Creator.

We are creatures of habit, and whatever habits of thinking, speaking, and envisioning that we have developed and practiced repeatedly will predominate at the time of our transition. However, if at the time you are ready to pass, you keep your mind on God, but you are not doing so now, more than likely you will not do it then. The principles of success are always the same whatever the goal. Whatever we desire, we must focus on it and build the consciousness that will draw it to us because we have that same vibration, the mental state that is the equivalent of the desire.

The book of Judas, one of the books lost to Christianity until it was found in Egypt in the 1970s, states that Jesus said, "Another realm exists beyond the material world, an immortal holy race above the mortal human race." The book of Thomas states, "God's kingdom is already here... only people do not see it." It later states that Jesus told his disciples: "The dead are not alive, and the living will not die." Living in ignorance are the walking dead; awakened souls, however, are always alive in the Spirit.

A wise person — a serious pleasure seeker — seeks to find his best options for eternal happiness, wherever that may be, and prepares for his next moment, his eternal future. He does so by becoming qualified to obtain and experience his heart's desires, by taking on a corresponding state of mind and emotion in this present moment. What I want you to know is that life is more than we may have realized is possible. Life abounds everywhere; it's not just what we can perceive with our limited physical senses. As Jesus said, "In my Father's house are many mansions: if it were not so, I would have told you. I go to prepare a place for you" (John 14:2).

Happiness and Prosperity Practices

A.　Observe what is happening in your life, and go back and remember its cause in a previous thought, desire, emotion, or action. Did you follow your heart and bliss, or your computer mind or the computer mind of others? Observe how many times you have changed in this life, and that you continue to exist; therefore, you are not the body but an eternal soul.

B. Contemplate and create your next life by being now how you want to be later. Use the following declarations: Today, I will feel love and bliss all the time, regardless of what is happening. Today, I will live my life as I choose to live it in the future. Today, I will behave as I want to behave in the future. Today, I will treat others in the manner in which I want others to treat me.

C. Act as if you are as you desire to be, and you will be: develop the consciousness, attitude, talents, and behavior that you desire to manifest in the future.

Prospering Mantras

Now I remember who I am and the divine, godlike powers I possess.
I am a spirit/soul on a mission of love.
I am eternal, for eternity is God and I am part of God.

CHAPTER SEVEN

The Pleasurable Way to Be Healthy and Vibrant

*H*ow we treat our bodies today will determine their condition in the future. A stroke twenty-two years ago was my wake-up call. I had two choices: I could turn the care of my body over to doctors, which would be enormously expensive and would subject me to many unknown, even dangerous, side effects from the medicines they would prescribe, or I could take responsibility for the health of my body temple. I chose the latter and have been happy ever since that I did. Looking forward to a life of prescription drugs, operations, and tasteless foods in meager quantity did not appeal to me, being the pleasure seeker that I am.

It wasn't just the excess of heavy, indigestible foods and alcohol that I had been consuming that set my body up for the stroke. My emotional and mental condition contributed too. I was suffering from shame and embarrassment as a result of criticism from others, who had been telling me all about the mistakes and failures they thought I had made in my ministry. Now I realize that these people felt envious toward me, but at the time I didn't think of this. Moreover, on top of my feelings of remorse and shame at the time was my old fear that I would lose my mate to another woman.

Waking up and finding myself in a hospital, I was surprised. The last thing I remembered was falling out of bed when my left side stopped working. I knew right away I would be fine, and my body did quickly return to normal functioning, but this event gave me a renewed appreciation for the importance of excellent health. The first thing I did was become vegetarian and eliminate from my diet the foods that had contributed to the stroke. Then I went on to learn that good health is economical, natural, and pleasurable. Sickness is expensive, unnatural, and miserable.

There is really no need for the body to be sick before we leave this world. It's possible to remain healthy up until the moment we leave our current body through the portal of death for our next adventure in enlightenment. And turning responsibility for any part of our lives, including our physical health, over to someone else is never a good idea.

No one cares as much as we do about what happens to us. We are the ones who suffer the pain and immobility of physical illness or the pleasure of a healthy, vibrant body, not our advisers. They have their own challenges. And we don't need to be medical doctors to know how to have healthy, happy bodies, minds, and emotions, or how to heal ourselves should there be a problem. Health professionals can still be of service to us, however. Finding the right one means doing some research and choosing the health facilitator who will work with us as a partner in attaining our health objectives.

Finding Our Way to Good Health

A woman dreamed that a monster was chasing her. In her dream the woman ran as fast as she could to escape the monster, until at last she came to a dead end and there was no way out. Out of breath, terrified, and helpless, she looked at the monster and said, "What are you going to do with me?"

"I don't know, lady," replied the monster, "it's your dream."

Like this woman, we are always afraid of what will happen to us — what will happen tomorrow, what will happen if I fail, what will happen if so-and-so leaves me, what will happen if I don't have the money I need, what will happen if I get sick, and on and on. We become fearful when we perceive the world through fear glasses, through layers of ignorance. But we can take off the fear glasses and view life as God created it: we can step out of our frightening dream. In reality, the world is beautiful, perfect, and harmonious. Our role is to live in harmony with the way Mother Earth and our bodies were designed to function.

Finding your way to good health will likely require some research on your part. As history tells us, geniuses do their own research to find answers to their questions. Often such courageous persons have been ridiculed, ostracized, or done away with to keep their findings secret. This is why we must be independent thinkers and do our own research, whatever the issue, including the issue of our health. Big, big, big money is made from people's sicknesses. Good health, like happiness, is almost free and is always available to everyone, as much of it as we desire.

Problems in life, physical and otherwise, come when we act as parrots instead of gods, repeating what we have heard or been taught, without using our divine intelligence and powers of logic and discernment to know what is true and what is false. When we do this, we must suffer the consequences of our misguided actions. The popular method of education is the parroting system. It rewards those who can parrot best what they have been taught, and punishes the independent thinkers and researchers. The body is simple to understand and take care of, and yet there is so much sickness, and more diseases are being identified daily that apparently never existed before. There are two possible reasons for this: either the medical profession is not fully aware of how the body functions, or it does not want people to know how simple it is to be healthy.

Life works simply. And so does health. Living in harmony with nature means good health, because the body is part of nature and operates by the same laws. The troubles that we are witnessing on the planet are the results of our consciousness and behavior, of our living in disharmony with nature. Likewise, no one's body gets sick for no reason; there is a cause. When we do not like the effect we are getting, we can find the cause of the problem, get rid of it, and do what works. When we do away with the cause, the effect must and will change. This is a basic law of the universe. The body, being part of nature, must operate in the same way as the rest of nature.

Bodies are amazing vehicles through which souls express themselves; they are temples of the living God. The body is an electrochemical carbon unit run by divine intelligence and influenced by our thoughts and emotions as well as the substances we put in it and on it. Interestingly enough, people may take excellent care of their cars, houses, furniture, and appliances, keeping them functioning well, but have little knowledge about the body. What good are those things if you cannot use them because the body won't function properly? Bodies need clean water, fresh and nourishing food, oxygen, and protection.

We make sure that the engines and gas lines of our cars are clean, but how many people keep their colons clean? The body absorbs nutrients from the food via the small intestine, and the colon eliminates the waste. But if the colon is caked with old feces, the body is being poisoned and the physical energy and vitality we need becomes depleted. In time, toxicity takes its toll by causing disease and chronic ailments. To date I have cleaned my liver thirty times; the liver performs over five hundred functions and is vital for health. I use *The Amazing Liver and Gallbladder Flush*, by Andreas Moritz, as my guide. Many people recommend using colloidal silver, taken as directed, for destroying all viruses in minutes. Do your own research and come to your own conclusions.

Good health and vitality are influenced by the following four elements: (1) our thoughts and emotions, (2) what goes into and on the body, (3) the body's activities, and (4) external circumstances. Holding on to grudges and resentments and seething with anger and envy lower our vibration and invite in lower-level energies that attack the body in the same way that we attract unsavory people by negative thinking. Ponder this: because we attract only those people, events, and conditions that match our frequency signature, when we keep our frequency signature as high as possible, nothing with a lower frequency, including viruses, people, and events, can enter our sphere. We are more powerful than anything in the universe, for we are spirits, godlike souls possessing the power of consciousness. For this reason, never give your faith or vote to any disease, person, or event that you do not want, because if you do, you will bring it into your life by giving it your soul power of manifestation.

Thoughts and Emotions Influence Our Health

Happy thoughts and loving feelings are beneficial for the body, and all negative emotions, such as resentment, anger, hatred, and guilt, are destructive to it. Negative emotions lead to illness because they close off the flow of inspiring thoughts and impede the flows of oxygen and blood to the brain and other organs, which they need in order to be healthy. These can also lead to poor judgment. Our unhappy thoughts and negative emotions make us feel bad, and in order to feel better at least for a while, we may consume foods or drinks or drugs that comfort us but also injure our health. Or, storming out of the house in an angry mood, we may be so preoccupied with our anger that we can't see or think straight and may get into a car accident.

We are pleasure seekers. Yet while we do not like pain, and we try to avoid it, we often end up creating it ourselves because we lack simple, basic knowledge of how the body functions and how we function as souls. When our minds torment us, we need to find a way to feel good. I used to drink excessive amounts of alcohol to feel better, to feel confident, and to have a good time by shutting off my unhappy mind. I really thought my unhappiness was the result of how others were treating me, when it was really the result of how I was treating myself. The desire for alcohol left me after I stopped judging myself as bad. I didn't like alcohol's side effects — the way my body felt after drinking and the way I screamed at people and was rude. I sincerely prayed to God to please take the desire for alcohol from me.

With compassion for myself, I stopped punishing myself with shameful feelings as if I were the worst person in the world. I gave up judging myself as bad and no longer labeled myself, or drinking alcohol, as bad. I realized that I had been drinking to feel good, and that afterward I would feel bad. When I stopped feeling guilty, ashamed, and bad, I no longer needed to drink to feel good, so the vicious cycle stopped. The only way out was to feel good all the time by flowing bliss — the secret solution to all problems and the cure for all unhappiness. Judgments of who and what are good and bad are simply the result of our cultural and religious conditioning and change depending upon the culture or religion. Using these judgments of good and bad to emotionally blackmail people into conforming to our will is abusive. Souls are tender, and we need to treat each person as precious and encourage him or her to bring forth their real nature as they learn to follow their own inner guidance even if this goes against our plans for them. Unconditional love is the key for building wonderful relationships. Creating an environment in which the people we love are able to freely be themselves is the greatest gift that we can offer to anyone anywhere: "Whatever you wish men to do for you, do likewise also for them; for this is the law and the prophets" (Matthew 7:12). The amazing gift in this is that whatever we offer others we are also offering to ourselves.

Soon after my prayer, and after I eliminated my guilt and shame connected with drinking and how I acted when intoxicated, I noticed that my desire for alcohol was gone, never to return. The Higher Power had intervened, and I was healed. I had asked and was humble enough to know that I could not do this on my own and needed the help of the Supernatural Power. Because we have free will, we must ask. Even God does not force himself on us by interfering with our free will, although the Supersoul knows everything and is always ready to help us when we ask.

"And, behold, they brought to him a man sick of the palsy, lying on a bed; and Jesus seeing their faith said unto the sick of the palsy; Son, be of good cheer; thy sins be forgiven thee.... And he arose, and departed to his house" (Matthew 9:2, 7). From this we can understand that our judgments of ourselves make us sick — mentally, emotionally, and also physically. When we accept forgiveness, meaning we release the flow of love that we stopped by our negative thoughts and emotions, then God who is love and bliss can express through us without obstruction, and naturally we are healed. "Being of good cheer" tells us to be happy and forget all the thoughts that we have been using to make ourselves miserable and sick.

JUDGING THESE BODIES

We can observe how people make themselves miserable by judging their bodies as not good enough. Others' criticisms were not my only problem. I also criticized myself. Oh, how I suffered from judging my body as not pretty enough and sexy enough to attract and keep the man I wanted. Every beautiful woman was a potential enemy, a threat to my happiness. A scenario like this pits a woman against other women, as if a man were the source of her happiness, good feelings, and survival. I thought I was my body, so my perception of it influenced how I felt and what I did.

Judging our bodies as not pretty enough, not good enough to receive love, protection, or the attention of another, leads to depression, especially when it appears that our plans to attract the person we believe will give us future happiness are destroyed. And if we engage in constant competition, nasty gossip, and mean-spirited activities to protect ourselves and whatever we believe is ours, this hardens our hearts and makes us mean and sharp-tongued, which makes us feel bad. As serious pleasure seekers, we

like to be happy, so it goes against our purpose to fall into negative emotions because of what anyone does or does not do.

We can stop such unhealthy behavior by learning to keep our
minds in the transcendental position, instead of constantly judging ourselves as good or bad. Such judgment keeps us in constant
anxiety, in which there is no peace and no bliss, because we stop
them in order to terrorize ourselves and others. Observe your
thoughts and feelings about your body and the bodies of others.
Notice which beliefs have been running, and perhaps ruining,
your life. You cannot control someone else's mind or actions, but
you can control your own mind and actions.

The solution to body problems, and all problems, is to learn
to be happy, deep down happy, at the core of our being. Shaming
ourselves because of the age, shape, color, sex, or condition of our
bodies does not make us beautiful by any standard. And it does
not make us happy; it can, however, make us seriously mentally ill
and physically sick. Emotional distress can lead to chemical imbal-
ances and substance dependencies, as well as to physical illnesses
and aberrations in our behavior. What we need to know is how
important our consciousness — what we think, believe, and feel
emotionally — is for excellent health. Even a virus has no effect on
the body if our immune system is strong enough and we do not
give the virus power through our beliefs and thoughts.

In addition to keeping a positive, enthusiastic attitude, we
must also avoid letting anything toxic enter the body, including
by injection. I got no inoculations before any of my travels to third
world countries, because I did not want to weaken my immune
system with dangerous drugs. Inoculations can have all sorts of
horrific side effects. The power of the spiritualized mind is great,

and simply by changing her attitude a person can slough off physical illness. One of the very best medicines is bliss combined with a positive mental attitude. Fear, stress, worry, grudges, and hate are more dangerous for the body than what others can do to us. All is consciousness, and this is true in every aspect of life.

Why stop feeling good in order to judge your body as too fat, too thin, too young, too old, too wrinkled, or too ugly? What is the value of self-torture? It does not change anything for the better, and it makes us self-destruct. A happy, smiling face that expresses affection and kindness is always the most beautiful. It's an expression of the soul radiating its brilliance and warmth.

Fear of future unhappiness because of what others may say about our bodies or do to us on account of our physical appearance keeps many of us from participating fully in life. Especially as the body ages, many people, even those who have been wonderful, highly successful entertainers, entrepreneurs, and humanitarians, hide away out of sight so that others will not judge their bodies. Even great souls sometimes give up under the pressure of gossip columnists and the cruel words of the envious. But while others may judge us unmercifully, what they think of us is none of our business. Our thoughts, feelings, and actions are our business.

Realize that, over time, all bodies change in appearance, beginning at the moment of conception. Everything made of matter goes through a cycle, beginning, continuing for a while, and disintegrating. Why look into the mirror each day and cry because your body does not look like it used to, or does not look as good as someone else's? Put a cloth over the mirror and forget about what the body looks like, or learn to enjoy the effects of time on the physical body. As we age, we must recognize that our senior years are meant for helping others with our wisdom and love, not for our complaints and litanies of losses. What benefits do we get from complaining? How do complaints give us bliss?

Stop perceiving yourself as a physical being and instead perceive yourself as a spiritual being beyond time or matter, and express yourself through your spiritual mind. Don't listen to people who criticize your body or tell you that you're useless or unwanted — they are up to no good and are seeking pleasure from your pain. God wants you and is sending unlimited amounts of love to you, but you must accept it to feel it. Be grateful that you have a body, take care of it so that it functions well, and go about your mission.

We are gods, already perfect, regardless of the stage of our earthly experience. We must avoid thinking or saying derogatory things about our own appearance and about the appearances of others, especially children. And we must not give others the power to make us sad or happy by their words and actions. You will stop doing so when you realize what you have been doing to yourself. It's our treatment of others and our thoughts that affect how much or how little happiness, that precious treasure, we experience.

What Goes into and on the Body Influences Our Health

And God said, "Behold, I have given you every herb yielding seed, which is upon the face of all the earth, and every tree which bears fruit yielding seed; to you it shall be for food. And to every beast of the earth and to every fowl of the air, and to everything that creeps upon the earth, wherein here is life, I have given every green herb for food; and it was so."

GENESIS 1:29–30

Chemicals applied to your body or found in the foods you eat affect your health. The skin is the largest organ of the body, and it absorbs whatever is applied, including, for example, poisons such as chlorine and fluoride. When we bathe or swim in chlorinated or fluoridated water, or drink it, these poisons are absorbed into our bodies. In time this has a detrimental effect, although for a while it may seem harmless. We are told that chlorine and fluoride are not a problem, so people tend to believe that these chemicals will not poison them. But a poison is a poison. Poisons are always dangerous and should be avoided. Boiling water for a few minutes can eliminate unfriendly bacteria, but to get rid of the other contaminants you will need to do some research. Remember to make sure your water-filtering system takes out what you do not want and keeps in what you do. Boiling water for twenty minutes will oxygenate and ionize the water. Keep the water hot in a thermos and drink from this all during the day to get the best results. Does it make sense to believe that putting poison in the water or in foods as they grow in the soil will make the body healthy?

EAT ONLY WHAT GOD CREATES PERFECTLY

Consider the many chemicals that may be found in the foods you eat, if you haven't already done so. The purer the food, the better it is for us. "If God didn't make it, don't eat it," is a good slogan to live by. What I mean by this statement is that any fruit, vegetable, nut, seed, or grain in its original form, without chemical additives and unnecessary processing and packaging, and that has been grown without pesticides and chemical fertilizers, is best for the body. Who knows more about what the body needs than the creator of the body? Just by eliminating all processed so-called foods, we can lower our grocery bills and our bodies will restore themselves to health. Doctors do not heal the body; the body heals itself when the source of the problem is removed. The body, like the universe, is a cause-and-effect machine. Change what's causing a health problem and the effect must change too. Stop doing what is causing the problem, and do what produces health naturally.

Simply by using common sense we can figure out that chemical-laced and processed foods harm the body and brain, so that the brain is not able to do its best work. The fact that these foods may appeal to our taste buds doesn't make them good for us. We're manipulated into wanting them. They are meant to be addictive so that we crave and buy them. Some manufacturers of processed foods hire scientists to develop additives that enable their products to capture our taste buds and addict us. These corporations then hire the most skilled psychologists to devise ad campaigns to sell their products, making sure that these products create the intense desire that motivates us to run out and buy them. The deck is stacked against us, and the house always wins, unless we know what is happening.

Any system that is invented, propped up, manipulated, controlled, and foisted on people by convincing them that fake is better than real is a scam. It may appear to be working for a while, but in time whatever is unnatural will create dis-ease, dysfunction, and breakdown. I remember when artificial, processed foods, and the philosophy that there is a pill and chemical for everything, found their way into the minds and buying habits of Americans in the 1950s. From this point on, obesity, allergies, autism, mental illness, and other food- and chemical-related illnesses and problems started increasing by leaps and bounds.

There was a big push to convince the public that processed and artificial are better than real. "Butter is bad, margarine is good," is one example of the erroneous propaganda foisted on us. We were told that butter was raising our cholesterol levels and creating heart attacks, and that chemicals made to taste like butter were better and safer. We became excited by all the processed foods available, thrilled that we were living in the modern age, the age of advanced technology. We felt sorry for people in "underdeveloped" countries who were living simple, happy, and healthy lives with their families and communities. Rejecting something that God made for us, something perfect for the body and mind, we chose to buy the lie of "new and improved." No one can improve upon God's creation; it is already perfect. Food grown organically with love is delicious, nutritious, and satisfying. Processed foods supply empty calories.

Prevention is the best medicine, and it's also the best form of health insurance: by investing in fresh, organically grown foods, we can prevent illness. Food is medicine as well. Chemical treatments for illnesses can harm us, which may make you wonder why they are promoted so heavily. To understand, ask yourself: Who is making money from sickness? Fear motivates us to agree to artificial solutions that do not actually heal us but increase our problems. Illness is nothing to fear, for we are divine beings with all godlike qualities. In healing ourselves, our challenge is to use what we have — our divine intelligence — to find out what will cure our illnesses, rather than give this power away to others who may not have our best interests in mind. Medical professionals who tell us that we are suffering from something incurable are really saying, "You will need to stay on medications that will only suppress the condition, for we don't make any money if you are healed." Our body is our responsibility. Before we accept anyone's word as law, it is a good idea to do our research and seek the opinions of a few trusted health professionals. I can give you an example of this from my own life. When I lived in India, my body developed rheumatoid arthritis. I suffered tremendously in my arms and hands. Wanting to know the cause and a natural cure for this, I did some research on the Internet, using the search phrase "cause and natural cure for rheumatoid arthritis." A huge amount of information appeared, but I found that certain facts were consistently reported throughout the sources I investigated. I applied what I learned, and the problem disappeared. That was five years ago. I stopped the cause of my illness, and the effect had to change. I once mentioned this experience to a physician who was riding with me in a van from the airport to a hotel in San Francisco. She asked me what drugs I was taking, and I told her none, that I had healed my body naturally. She turned her face away and did not speak another word to me. You see, her specialty was rheumatoid arthritis.

Also be aware that some doctors may recommend unnecessary surgery for certain health problems. For example, some people have their gallbladders removed — as if the body doesn't need the gallbladder to function properly — when perhaps all that is necessary is to remove stones from them. This can be done with a simple liver cleansing, by ingesting apple juice, olive oil, and lemon juice. Natural remedies that work have been in existence forever but are often put down as old wives' tales — implying that old wives don't know what they're doing.

Whenever a health problem occurs, do your research to find the cause — and there is a cause — and eliminate it. Do not rush into doing anything; wait until you are certain it is your best option. I recommend a two-step plan that always works: stop doing whatever is causing the problem, and start doing what works to give you the results you desire. If, for example, you are having colon problems, clean your colon, and then find out which foods clog the colon and avoid them.

God's medicine consists of fresh, organically grown foods, clean water, sunshine, fresh air, movement of the body, and positive, loving feelings and thoughts. Investigate your health problems on the Internet, in books, by talking to friends who have overcome the same physical problems, and by seeking advice from trusted health professionals who adhere to the natural path. These dedicated and sincere health professionals have some amazing healing techniques available. Keep in mind that ethical people do not terrorize you or make you feel like a fool too stupid to make your own decisions.

The Ayurvedic system is the best all-around system for health and vitality. It recommends specific delicious foods, as well as offers recipes, to suit each particular body type and each condition to be healed. Illness is caused by imbalance, and Ayurvedic medicine focuses on rebalancing the ailing body. Homeopathy is another excellent system for prevention and healing. Use allopathic, or Western, medicine only for emergencies, for its methods primarily entail drugs and surgery.

FOOD OF THE GODS

What could be better than real cream that is organic and raw? Combine this with raw chocolate and organic cane sugar, and you have an awesome dessert in thirty seconds that is completely satisfying. How about a mango lassi? Lassi is made of organic yogurt and mango whipped in the blender, with some organic sugar added. Most people are missing the sweetness of life. Do not believe that raw sugar, raw honey, maple syrup, and other natural, organic, and unprocessed sweeteners are bad for the body, or that chemical, synthetic sweeteners (and creamers) for coffee are good. Aspartame, a chemical sweetener, is known to reduce intelligence, and many believe it causes brain tumors and Alzheimer's disease. Agave syrup, on the other hand, is a natural sweetener with only a few calories, and stevia is a natural sweetener that has no calories.

Observe the connection between what people are eating and drinking and using in their homes and what is happening to the health of their bodies and the health of the planet. We are part of one system; what is happening to one part affects all the parts. Your common sense will tell you the truth about what works to produce health and what causes sickness. Nothing happens by accident, and there is always a cause for every effect. Results don't lie.

Walk down the aisles of most any supermarket and take a look at what's being offered. What can you find that is really fit to eat, drink, or use in your home — what won't make the body and mind sick in time? Many foods are packaged in plastic containers, whose poisonous constituents leach into the food packed inside. You'll also find adulterated milk products, which have been pasteurized and homogenized, and which cause consumers to develop lactose intolerance. Raw organic milk from happy cows is a wonder food and delicious. Rancid grains create allergies and are carcinogenic. Phony ice cream that contains no actual milk and bears a list of chemicals we cannot even pronounce is as good for the body as eating a Styrofoam cup.

The only real food in the market will be found in the produce department. But most of this food has been grown with pesticides, artificial fertilizers, and genetically altered seeds. Open your eyes, and you will be amazed. Read the real story behind massproduced and processed foods and you will be confused, perhaps even angry. Then you will want to return to a wealthy, healthy lifestyle, your inheritance, available to you and your precious children since the beginning.

Fruit drinks made of fresh berries and other fruits taste fabulous and contain antioxidants. Why ingest a carbonated drink concocted with artificial flavors and chemicals, which may taste something like an orange or lemon, but doesn't include any fruit? Eat an orange or make lemonade, and get the full flavor and health benefits and save money.

Our Body's Activities Influence Our Health

Forget about using the word *exercise*. I prefer the term *move the body*, because *exercise* carries with it the connotation of pain and struggle. Move the body. Ignore the elevator and walk upstairs, except when you have a heavy load. Do your own housework. Walk around the block and talk with your neighbors, or at least smile and say hello. Jump in a lake, river, or ocean and swim. Carry your own groceries to the car. Park a distance from where you want to go so that you can walk to it, swinging your arms to cleanse the lymph glands. Plant a garden: think of all the work you can do with your body as you produce an abundant crop of flowers, fruits, and vegetables. And try yoga. Yoga has served me well over the years, and I've developed my own system that works for me — you can do the same for yourself.

When you first start to exercise, whether you engage in an exercise regime or just start walking regularly, don't torture yourself. I like the baby-step method myself: a little each day, and sometimes more. Too much strenuous anything is not natural and can wear out body parts prematurely, although occasionally a strenuous workout is fine. We need to walk briskly for only ten to fifteen minutes a day to keep the heart strong. Look for new ways to get some exercise. Go out dancing with your sweetheart or friends. I like going to the Hindu temple down the street, where people worship by chanting, singing, and dancing for God. At home, I frequently exercise in another way. My office is on the second floor, and I choose to have only one phone in the house. When the phone rings and I am downstairs, I have five rings to make it to the top. I run up and down the stairs all day while answering the phone. It's fun and healthy, and I save money by having just one phone.

Sloth, or laziness, is one of the seven deadly sins because the body is designed for moving. The more sedentary we become, the less motivated we are to do anything, and our vitality, creativity, and enthusiasm slip away. What we don't use atrophies. Lack of physical activities makes the body rigid, and it becomes painful to dance or even walk. If this describes you, do what you can to get moving again, even if it means simply walking across the room. This is enough to start the rectification process. Each day walk across the room and then go a little bit farther than before. Soon, if you continue this baby-step process, your body will become strong again.

STRENGTHEN THE BODY

Whenever we have a health problem, instead of treating the specific problem we should develop the habits of health. Years ago I had excruciating lower back pains. When I finally went to a chiropractor to find out what was wrong, he told me I would probably need to go to a back specialist and have an operation. Having an operation on my back was not my idea of a good time, so I chose the natural path instead. I hired a yoga teacher to come to my home three days a week and work out with me. Knowing myself, I was certain that I wouldn't go to a yoga studio or gym, as this was not my nature. I was also a procrastinator. (Awareness of our weaknesses helps us to work around them and not be stopped by them.)

Good health, success, loving relationships, and prosperity are all about having good habits. Never focus on what you want to get rid of, for this locks in the problem. Focus on what you want instead, and then build that habit one baby step at a time. The yoga teacher set up a workout program of yoga and other movements for me, including dancing. She arrived at my home three mornings a week, and we worked the program together. Repetition creates habits, and soon I liked my workout program and gained strength in my lower back. One morning as I got out of bed, I noticed the pain was gone, completely, never to return. I had also stopped wearing the three-inch-high heels that had thrown my back out of alignment. The natural circulation of energy had been blocked, causing distortion and pain.

Pain indicates an energy blockage. When I permitted the energy to flow freely once again, my health and vitality were restored. When we allow our soul feelings of love and bliss to flow, we are happy, and when the energy channels in the body are unblocked and the energy is flowing freely, the body is healthy. Remember the axiom "As above, so below," which tells us how everything in the material world works, including the body, which is made of material energy. My body was healed without an operation or further treatment.

External Circumstances Influence Our Health

Something unforeseen can happen to the body that has nothing to do with our thinking, eating, drinking, or other activities. Remember the five influences on every manifestation? One of them is nature, which includes creatures. A brown recluse spider bit my leg, causing it to swell up more than twice its normal size. The poison began killing the flesh of that leg, putting me in a wheelchair and making me almost delirious. I decided to visit the emergency room at a nearby hospital. The nurse there told me that, unless I checked in immediately, the leg would have to be amputated, and that if it were not amputated I'd be dead in two weeks.

I don't allow myself to be frightened into doing anything, unless it's to run away quickly from a possibly dangerous situation. I left the hospital immediately, as this had all the earmarks of a dangerous situation. I went home and did a natural Ayurvedic remedy, and my leg was almost well in seven days. It took a couple of weeks more for the healing to be complete. You need to know what you are doing when you take matters into your own hands, however. I have studied and practiced good health and natural forms of healing for many years.

Almost daily I hear about miracles concerning people who were told they would never walk again, or whose physical condition was hopeless for some other reason. As I noted earlier, if you develop an illness, find out what others have done in the same situation to heal themselves. Always follow your conscience. Now if I notice I have a health problem, first I meditate and ask the Supersoul, God Within, to tell me the cause of the problem and the natural cure. Immediately this knowledge is given to me, because who knows more than God? Every healing modality has its place, and it is up to us to know how to use them and not be used by them. When we abdicate our responsibility, as if we were powerless, we must take what we get and not complain.

Sacred Living

Health is about living in harmony with Mother Nature and being conscious of who we are as spiritual beings. Life can either be a mundane experience in which we go through the motions, or it can be a sacred experience full of joy and blessings. In ancient times, people celebrated the changing of the seasons, they made offerings to God of flowers and fruits, and they were aware of the symbiotic relationship between humans, the animals, plants, nature spirits, and higher beings.

Our homes can be sacred temples of love that provide us with sanctuary. Flowers and beautiful pictures that make us feel relaxed and peaceful, and remind us of the perfection of God's creation, turn our homes into spiritual environments, miniature heavens on earth. Our places of business too can be transformed into temples, where we worship God by helping others be happy, healthy, and prosperous through our services and products. If you are on a mission for God, then your work is your ministry. Put positive life-affirming and success-oriented statements on the walls so your mind is absorbed in truth and you feel good being there. Our bodies are temples of the living God, for the Supersoul is with us. Keep the body clean inside and out and free of dis-ease. Dress in a pleasing way that makes you feel good and honors your path, work, and message.

Grow a Garden

Build and care for a garden with your children, grandchildren, other family members, and friends. Plant your favorite flowers on your balcony if this is all you have. Dig up the useless grass in the yard and put in your garden, or at least do so in a few areas for starters, as this will surprise the neighbors. When your plants start producing food, your neighbors will want to do the same. (If they ridicule you, remember that, although ridicule may come first from doubting minds, in time the courageous are admired and copied.) Plant dwarf fruit and nut trees too, and you will have an abundance of fruit in just three years. Remember: you do have a future, and three years will pass anyway, whether you plant trees or not.

There is no better way for children to learn about how life works than to work in the garden. Whether we are adult or child, woman or man, gardens work with us to build the character, self-esteem, and confidence we need. We will always have enough of these when we tend the garden — and having them leads to good health. You can even create your own seed bank of organic seeds for future plantings.

Avoid using toxic products in your garden, because whatever goes into the soil goes into the food and then into the body. Cow manure free of poisons and other chemicals is the best fertilizer, and it draws nature spirits in some mystical way. Earthworms are fabulous, for they turn garbage and cow manure into topsoil, the very best growing medium possible. The Rodale Press has published many books on organic gardening.

Have a cow if you can. Given how far we are from living in harmony with nature, having a cow may seem like an absurd suggestion. But real wealth in this world is land, an abundant supply of drinkable water, and cows. Whatever happens, everything we need for a life of abundance Mother Earth provides. While living in India for four years, I tended cows and learned about their importance to the balance and prosperity of the earth and her inhabitants. Cows generously give us milk, which is used to make yogurt, buttermilk, sour cream, cream, butter, ice cream, cheese, and cottage cheese. Cow urine is medicinal, and cow dung can be used as fertilizer or dried and used like firewood to cook our food and heat our homes. When the cow dies naturally, its remains are useful to human beings.

We have been programmed to believe that milk is bad for the body, but it is pasteurized and homogenized milk that is bad for the body. They make milk indigestible. Unless the milk comes from cows that are cared for with love, milk is harshly taken from the mother cow. (Her baby is also taken from her, as if cows do not have feelings or the right to live a happy and safe life.) Better to practice veganism and avoid all milk products to avoid hurting cows and our bodies. Milk is the blood of the mother cow transformed by her love for her baby. How could any creature who is able to turn blood into delicious milk, cream, and butter by her love not have feelings? All animals have feelings, and we are their caretakers. We must not for any reason be their abusers. Whatever we do to others, including animals, will be done to us, if not now, then in our next lifetime. Karma follows us, and no one can escape the reactions to his actions.

Good health is simply a process of alignment and balance that comes from acting harmoniously with the way Mother Earth functions. When we understand how nature works, we know how the body works, and when we know how the body works, we know how nature works — for everything works by the same laws of nature. Nothing in life is complicated unless we make it complicated. Sacred living offers us our best options for happiness, love, vitality, beauty, fun, and adventure. God made everything perfect in every way, just for us.

Happiness and Prosperity Practices

A. Observe the quality of the food and drink that you take into your body. Was it created by God, or was it processed, making it capable of causing a breakdown in the body, emotions, and intelligence? Observe that the body is a magnificent machine and must be taken care of in order to function at its optimal level. Observe whether you make yourself feel bad, guilty, or ashamed as a result of your food and drink choices, or because of your feelings about the size or features of your body temple.

B. Contemplate what you have been taught about your body. Have you allowed yourself to feel bad because of your body or what others have said about your body? If so, why are you doing this to yourself? Use the following declarations: Today, I will feel good regardless of what I eat and drink. Today, I will sincerely pray and ask God to eliminate the desire for any food, drink, or other substance that can harm my body. Today, I refuse to feel guilt and shame for what I have eaten or consumed. Today, I will dance to at least one song and take a walk while chanting my prospering mantras.

C. Act as if you are as you desire to be, and you will be: select food and drink in its natural, unprocessed form as Mother Earth grew it. Prepare the food with love as an offering to Mother/Father God. Then receive the food, say a prayer of gratitude, and enjoy it as a gift from God. (This raises the vibration of the food and drink and heals your body, mind, and emotions.)

Speak kind and loving words about your body and give up judging the bodies of others or yours as good or bad.

Prospering Mantras

Every day in every way, my body is becoming healthier and more energetic.

I am not the body; I have a body.

I bless my body and feel affection for every cell.

CHAPTER EIGHT

Entrance into the Realm of Divine Pleasures

*E*ntrance into the realm of divine pleasures happens automatically when we perceive the world, others, and ourselves with spiritual vision. Spiritual means God, the Creator, as distinct from God's creation. Material scientists are absorbed in the study of the creation, but spiritual scientists prefer to be absorbed in learning about and having a relationship with the Creator. Spiritual scientists have it all. The spiritual world and material world are similar and also different — the spiritual world is blissful and opulent because it is the kingdom of God, where God lives with us and all the inhabitants are in love with God and each other. The material world is our perception of the spiritual world, not as it really is, but how the spiritual world appears to us through a filter made of layer upon layer of fear- and lack-based conditioning devoid of the presence of God, the Great Spirit.

Although the mind is spiritual and designed to reflect the opulent kingdom of God, everything is distorted in our minds when we perceive the world through this dark, clouded filter. This is why we cannot trust our minds to tell us the truth, but we can trust our conscience and direct revelations from God Within. Sacred knowledge passed down to us from messengers sent from God is our saving grace, for with it we can once again know who we are as spiritual beings, make God the center and purpose of our lives, and start living again in the realms of divine pleasures. The Bhagavad Gita tells us: "When one's intelligence, mind, faith, and refuge are all fixed in the Supreme, then one becomes fully cleansed of misgivings through complete knowledge and thus proceeds straight on the path of liberation" (5.17).

God is all there is. Everything exists within God, and all souls are part of God and, consequently, persons. In the spiritual world, everyone and everything is a person, self-luminous, conscious, and eternal, including trees, flowers, and other plants; insects and other animals; water; and fire. And of course Mother Earth is a person, as is the Sun, all planets are persons, and even the air is a person.

We may have been taught that only those with human bodies are persons and never wondered why and how these other creature bodies were alive, functioning perfectly, and moving. But what makes those nonhuman bodies move, grow, and perform their functions in the grand scheme of life other than spiritual beings inside working them? Souls are atomic in size and so can fit into any size body. Some people go so far as to decide that even humans are not people deserving of love and kindness if they do not belong to a certain religion, race, or other group. Native Americans who follow the ancient spiritual teachings of their elders also accept the personage of creatures and elements, as do the practitioners of Vedic wisdom. The Srimad Bhagavatam, which recounts the story of Lord Krishna, tells us: "God is the soul of the principle of goodness! The incarnations of that principle are innumerable! As thousands of watercourses come out of one inexhaustible fountain of water, so these incarnations are but emanations of that infinitely good energy of God which is full at all times" (1.3.26).

Clive Baxter, who is cited in the book *The Secret Life of Plants*, by Peter Tompkins and Christopher Bird, found that plants have feelings and respond to us and our thoughts and emotions. The plant is the garment for the soul that is having the plant experience. Similarly, an elephant is not just an animal: there is a soul within the body of the elephant. I especially like true stories that tell about acts of great love, intelligence, and devotion performed by animals. One such story is that of an elephant that lived at a Vedic temple in India, and whose job it was to carry out various functions for the temple during the worship services. After many years of faithful service, one day the elephant walked by himself to the steps of the temple, bent down on his front knees, put his head down in prayerful respect, and left his body. We've all read heroic stories of dogs, pigs, cats, and other animals saving people from death. Dogs are popular companions for many people because they do not judge their caretakers but accept them unconditionally.

All of us exist as contributors, for giving and receiving are the activities of souls. Each of us is serving someone or something all the time, even if this means only that our tongue is serving to taste delicious foods. Without the cycle of serving and being served, giving and receiving, there would be no life, for all of life operates in the same way that God gives to his beloved Goddess and she gives to her beloved. We are the lovers of God engaged in the process of eternal reciprocation and, in this way, reaching ever-increasing levels of bliss and opulence. But if we do not honor our nature, we stagnate, we fall into despair for lack of substance, for lack of love — and we live on love, the food and sustainer of souls.

Many years ago I was asked to be on a television program, *Lifestyles of the Rich and Famous*. I decided to watch one of the programs. The host was interviewing a man who had been a waiter and who, after saving his money, had bought his first restaurant, followed by another and another, and so on. At the time of the interview, he owned many five-star hotels and restaurants throughout Europe. The host of the program asked him, "Are you afraid you could lose all this enormous wealth that you have?" The man replied with a smile on his face, "Oh no! I'm a waiter." You see, he knew the art of service, so the loss of money was not important to him. He knew he could make more money, as much as he wanted, by serving people. Obviously, his level of service was excellent, which kept his customers coming back to his establishments. He treated his customers as the most important people in the world. The Bhagavad Gita tells us: "One who sees the Supersoul in every living being and equal everywhere does not degrade himself by his mind. Thus he approaches the transcendental destination" (13.29). Spiritual vision means that we look past the form that is covering each soul and recognize the real, live, feeling person inside, and that we treat her with kindness and respect.

Once we understand that spiritual life is about being who we are in the kingdom of God, which is everywhere, then everywhere we walk is holy ground. Mother Earth is blessed by our divine presence, and she is blessing us. We never leave the spiritual world: it is everywhere when we have spiritual vision and observe the sacredness of all of life. We are never separated from our Beloved, who is always with us and loves us beyond measure. God is everywhere, and we are like fish swimming in the ocean but not noticing the ocean because that is all there is.

Being devoid of God-consciousness is a frightening experience, because then we feel alone and believe we must struggle for survival, thinking that whatever we desire is in scarce supply, and that only the fittest, the most powerful, and the cruel will make it and be able to enjoy some measure of comfort and pleasure. Fear abounds when we are mentally and emotionally separated from our Source. I always tell my students: "Working for and with God will make you rich and happy." Living in the material world is a miserable condition fraught with difficulties and disappointments of all sorts, whereas living in the spiritual world is blissful. It's the same world, viewed from different perspectives.

Our major challenge is to maintain our spiritual state of mind and view of life when others do not have our same awareness and believe that their fear- and lack-based conditioning is true, and that our beliefs are false and foolish. Have compassion for them, for they have been co-opted by prophets of doom and consider themselves to be intelligent, when they have a poor fund of knowledge of the All and Everything. The mind is strong and has been in charge for a long, long time.

Only a person who is fixed in her true spiritual identity and a loving, reciprocal relationship with her God/Goddess within is able to hold her own and flow the river of God's love regardless of what others are saying or doing or world conditions. This takes practice, for we are creatures of habit, and habits are developed through repetition. For this reason, we must use this same system of repetition to develop the habits of thinking that will bring us what we desire and repel what we don't want.

Enlightened souls who are mystics tend to live in secluded

areas in order to maintain their spiritual consciousness and not be influenced by the disturbed minds of others. We may think that they are lonely, but as our loving relationship with our God within is developed through the practice of meditation, prayer, and awareness, what we call our alone time becomes our favorite and most satisfying and pleasurable time. From the moment we shift our awareness from the outer world of effects to the Spirit that is creating the outer world, and start perceiving the souls within bodies as the real persons, and the bodies as outer garments covering the soul bodies, we are fixed in the ultimate reality. The Bhagavad Gita tells us, "One who sees the Supersoul accompanying the individual soul in all bodies and who understands that neither the soul nor the Supersoul is ever destroyed, actually sees" (13.28).

Using Our One Vote

How do we protect ourselves from negative energy, help others to also be happy, and raise the frequency of the planet? It's a good idea to avoid people who are trying to convince you to believe in their limited, fear-based concepts. Consciousness is contagious, and because of this we must train ourselves to keep our minds quiet and not grab onto their words and believe them, unless we want those concepts to manifest for us. Be your happy and enthusiastic self and hold this state of transcendence regardless, and your outer world will change in time to match your consciousness.

There are people who emanate a continual stream of angry and resentful emotions as a way to manipulate others, but these negative emotions block their own good fortune. Because of this, of course, the movie screen of their lives reflects their state of mind back to them, which increases their negative emotions and fear. What I've noticed is that, unless we are alert to how attitude is transferable and, therefore, trouble is transferable, we will give up our friendly and enthusiastic attitude when we are around them and will lower our vibration to match theirs. It doesn't matter if they don't like us. What matters is our attitude and that we feel love and wish them well. Let them take on your affectionate and cheerful attitude, but if they don't, remember to continue to be yourself, your godly self, and spread your enthusiasm seeds wherever you go.

We help others by being as enlightened as possible. We must avoid the angry, envious, and resentful as best we can, or, by our regular association with them, some of their energy vibration can contaminate us like a disease. These are the subtleties of the influence that others can have on us unless we understand this process and rise above it and hold our own in the spiritual zone. Generally speaking, people are either hankering for something they do not have or lamenting over what they lost or did not attain. What a misuse of a beautiful mind and life.

The questions any serious pleasure seeker should ask are: What is the best use of my one vote, my power of choice? What can I do that will give me the greatest pleasure, happiness, and good fortune, now and forever? Jesus gave us the formula: "And he answering said, Thou shalt love the Lord thy God with all thy heart, and with all thy soul, and with all thy strength, and with all thy mind; and thy neighbor as thyself" (Luke 10:27). When we treat others as important — and they are — and we avoid judging them as bad in order to feel good ourselves, then people feel good around us and want to be with us.

Take Responsibility for It All

The mirror of the outer world can reflect only what we have contained within our consciousness. Jesus taught this lesson when he said to a crowd that was ready to kill a woman accused of adultery by stoning her: "He that is without sin among you, let him cast a stone at her" (John 8:7). No one came forth, and all dropped the stones they had been carrying and walked away.

The minds of most people are absorbed in labeling others as bad and glorifying themselves as good and better. No one wants to feel bad, so we project what we did or are doing onto others and call them bad and despicable in order to make ourselves appear innocent and good. Once we are honest with ourselves and recognize that whatever we have been judging others for is what we too have done, although perhaps on a smaller scale compared to their actions, then the outer projection will fade, for we've learned our lesson. Perhaps in a past life we did what we've judged others for, or just thought about it but never did it physically; still it was in our consciousness. Hating presidents, rulers, corporate leaders, bankers, priests, those of a different religion or nationality, parents, neighbors, mates, or whomever we believe is responsible for what is happening to us makes them into our devils who torment us when we torment ourselves.

Remember that there is no greater terrorist weapon or virus worse than your own mind running amock. Praying that misguided people who are committing cruelties against other souls become love-realized will help to bring this about; cursing and hating them only gives the negative more power. Studies have shown that groups of people praying and meditating on love and peace have positive effects: they can change what appear to be dire situations into pleasant and life-affirming situations. The biggest problem in the world is projecting hate-based thoughts to anyone, including God and ourselves.

When the will of God is established on earth, both nature and human society function justly, harmoniously, and happily. When our actions align with unconditional love, they bring freedom from harm and we attain our true nature. Then we are liberated from material world problems and receive spiritual world blessings that have always been available but that await our recognition.

There are three steps by which to rectify the world according to its heavenly ideal. First, we must understand that others are reflecting back to us something that is contained within our consciousness. This is where the power to change all personal and global conditions lies. Once we realize that whatever we judge others for, we have done or are doing, we no longer need to have that part of our consciousness take form in our relationships or what is happening in our world. It's like the universe is a mirror reflecting back to us our consciousness so that we can eliminate anything that is not love-based but fear- and lack-based. Everything is seeking balance. For this reason when we think of doing something or we do something abusive or dishonest, we set the pendulum swing to that direction, and the pendulum must, in order for balance and harmony to be restored, swing to the other side. We get back and experience what we sent out or caused someone else to experience. When we find the cause within our consciousness we can ask forgiveness from our God, although God is not judging us, and then stop judging ourselves or others. Once balance is restored, the outer reflection in our relationships and environment is of harmony and balance. Health is a matter of balance. Dis-ease is a matter of imbalance and disharmony. We can judge righteously — meaning, we can understand the differences between right actions that produce harmony and wrong actions that produce disharmony — but we do not indulge in judging others as good and bad, as if something is wrong with others or with us. Remember that school allows for mistakes but instead of a red pencil mark through our answer when it is wrong, the event takes place in our world as our test and lesson. Perhaps your schoolteacher punished you for your mistakes, but do not project the way people behave onto God.

There are no bad souls. The second step by which to rectify the world is to understand that, when we accept forgiveness for all the thoughts, words, fantasies, and actions that we judge others for, and then also forgive them, we are released from the karma associated with the act, and the outer reflection must change. The third step is to behave in a way that is harmonious with the laws of nature and the Divine, to recognize our soul nature as a god whose purpose is to love and serve our God and others for their pleasure. As pleasure seekers, we are also pleasure givers. Our challenge is to remember who we are, keep the mind spiritualized, and go forth with our plans and work with enthusiasm. (The word *enthusiasm* comes from the Greek phrase *en theos*, meaning "with God.")

Prophecies

Right now there are many predictions of war, plagues, disastrous earth changes, poverty, and the end of the world. First, let us understand something about prophecies. Anyone can predict whatever they want. The future is not set in stone, but is liquid and constantly changing, even as you read this. If anything you have read in this book so far has inspired and influenced you to increase your feelings of love and bliss, your future has been upgraded to a higher level of good fortune. When you give your vote — the creative power of your soul — to prophecies of disaster, you, along with others who are also contributing the power of their votes to the prophecies, are manifesting what could not happen otherwise.

Never believe what others are saying or predicting, no matter who they are or the position they hold, unless you want their predictions to come true. The fluid future is in a constant state of reordering itself to reflect our individual consciousness and the collective consciousness of all humans on the planet. More often than not, a prediction or dream only reflects the intention and attitude of the person making the prophecy — that is all. Basic metaphysics tells us that we are cocreators through our thoughts, desires, words, and activities. These creative abilities give us more power than anyone's prophecy. No one has a more direct line to God than you do, regardless of their public relations plan to build their credibility in your mind. I determine what's right for me by what my conscience, God Within, is telling me, and also by holding up the prophecy and statement to the light of divine logic and the laws of nature to reveal the truth of the claim.

From my research, I have concluded that our future is wonderful, more wonderful than one could possibly imagine. Although something wonderful is always happening, there is an extra boost of good fortune coming our way. Scientists are noticing many anomalies in the solar system that seem to point to something enormous taking place in the cosmos and influencing our solar system and Mother Earth. Perhaps you have read about the Mayan calendar coming to an end, the prophecies of end times, and the doom and gloom of the predictions of Nostradamus, the astrologer. But are these true?

First of all, endings are always in progress, making way for new beginnings, just as beginnings give way for endings: this is how material energy works. Everything in the universe operates in cycles. Each cycle of action starts, continues for a while, and then stops as the next cycle starts, continues for a while, and stops. One cycle flows into the next, just as spring flows into summer, summer into fall, fall into winter, winter into spring, and so on. One thought flows into the next thought, and one moment into the next. Our physical bodies go through cycles because they are made of material, earthly elements. The universe goes through major and minor cycles, but each cycle works by the same principles.

According to Vedic cosmology, we are currently in the Kali yuga — the winter season of a minor cycle. *Yuga* is Sanskrit for "cycle." The Kali yuga marks the end of a larger yuga cycle, just as winter is the end of a yearlong cycle of earth seasons, but also the precursor to spring — new life. We are preparing for the advent of the next golden age, the Satya yuga, the age of goodness and opulence abounding. You can witness the process of cycles in your garden. But souls do not go through cycles of material energy; only the outer garments of matter that drape our soul bodies go through these cycles. This is why I suggest to my students that they do not identify their bodies as themselves, or they will suffer as the material body goes through these cosmic cycles. We are at the dawning of a new golden age that is appearing before its appointed time for some divine reason, perhaps a special dispensation by the grace of God and heralded by the avatars Lord Jesus two thousand years ago and Lord Caitanya only five hundred years ago.

Within a few years, at the time indicated by the end of the Mayan calendar, our solar system will line up with the center of the galaxy, as it does once every twenty-six thousand years.

The Golden Age Is upon Us, Rejoice

Five hundred years ago — a few years before the time when Nostradamus (1503–66) was predicting catastrophic earth changes, wars, and horrific events, including the destruction of the earth — Caitanya (1486–1534), a holy man from India, prophesied a ten-thousand-year golden age, a time of a spiritual renaissance when unconditional love, beauty, and rejoicing in the opulence of all good fortune and mystic powers is celebrated.

Nostradamus predicted only violence and suffering, which in itself is strange and suspect. Why would I choose to believe in anything that I do not want to have happen, when, by doing so, I use my mystic powers of manifestation to create it? I have placed my faith in the prophecy of Caitanya, not in the prophets of doom and the lords of chaos, who must have our agreement and faith in order to manifest anything. We have nothing to lose by agreeing with Caitanya's prediction, and everything to gain; we have nothing to gain from believing the predictions of the astrologer Nostradamus and other prophets of doom, and everything to lose.

Remember, each of us has only one vote, and in order to pull something off on a global level, the masses must be convinced. Historically, they were convinced by fear and the prophecies of Nostradamus, an adept astrologer who understood the cycles of the cosmos. The only thing that is predestined is the predetermined mind-set of the people. You say, "But his prophecies came true, so he did know." Anything is possible when you get large numbers of people to agree with and believe in your prophecies. People who want these prophecies to appear to be true interpret them in that light. Others, up to no good, commit acts of violence in the ways and at the times predicted, and these appear to be those prophecies coming true. Our only problem has been: WE HAVE NOT KNOWN WHO WE ARE AND THE POWERS WE POSSESS. Someone who controls your mind and emotions controls your actions and thus your life and what happens to you.

Instead of being actors, and doing what they feel guided to do based on love and spiritual truths, most people are reactors who believe everything they are told when it comes to future disasters and conditions of lack and limitation. But when it comes to eternal truths about who they really are and what is possible for them, they do not believe, and they call the prophets of love and good fortune fools. We tend to parrot what we have been taught by people parroting what they have been taught by people parroting what they have been taught, and on and on. It takes a brave heart, a courageous person to learn and apply sacred teachings regardless of what the masses are programmed to believe. This is why there have been so few great souls. Every soul is greatness personified and a genius in potential, but many are latent in actualization.

Lord Jesus and Caitanya were not harbingers of fear, but bringers of the light of sacred knowledge and the solution to all problems, great and small, and bringers of the unconditional love of God and others. Lord Caitanya, like Jesus, taught people who we are as spiritual beings and how to attain supreme pleasure of the soul while still in one's current body. He taught us about the superior spiritual world of eternal life, where death does not exist and neither does poverty or any other material-world problem. This spiritual world he called Vaikunta, a Sanskrit word meaning "without anxiety," and it offers unlimited soul pleasures beyond what is possible in the lower-frequency realms of gross matter. We ascend to the higher realms when we graduate from the lower realms, and we graduate when we know who we are. At that time we become God-conscious and are fully engaged in being our true selves.

Caitanya, like Jesus, performed amazing miracles, which you can read about in *Caitanya Bhagavata* by Vrndavana Dasa Thakura and in other books about him, if you are interested. Historians say Caitanya's seven-foot-tall golden body was beautiful beyond description. He led a spiritual revival in India that is still recognized and celebrated by Vaisnavas, his followers throughout the world who practice his teachings. His message was simple: sing the holy names of Mother/Father God with love and devotion and enjoy ecstatic, supreme pleasure, the goal of life. He was called the Golden Avatar, because his advent into the world ushered in the dawning of the golden age of heaven on earth. Lord Jesus, in prayer, asked that, "as it is in Heaven, so it would be on Earth," as this was his mission. This is what is coming, not what the lords of chaos have been claiming, unless you choose to believe them. Each of us has free will and can choose to believe whatever we like, so choose your best options.

You Can Trust Yourself

Remember that, just because many people believe something, that does not make it true. We must always compare whatever we read, hear, or believe with the truth of our conscience. Does it feel good and right in your heart? Our conscience is our God Within (Emanuel), who is guiding and giving us new revelations. And we must trust our conscience above and beyond anyone or anything else. We feel the truth. We have always known it, but have been told that we do not know what's true, and that only they, whoever *they* are, know. When we follow the advice of others, unless those people demonstrate by their behavior what we want to attain, we become as lost and bewildered as they are.

That religion is the purest which gives us the purest idea of the sweetness, beauty, mercy, and grace of God/Goddess. We must explore beyond the cultural, political, and religious programming that is protected by force and threats of ostracism, ridicule, and punishment, including eternal hell. The highest spiritual teaching requires an absolute conception of our own spiritual nature. Help from on high is always available to us when we ask.

A New World Is Evolving

A whole new world is coming forth, which means there will be a great rise in the energy frequency of Mother Earth. Sit back, develop unconditional love, be kind, and enjoy the ride. Focus the power of your thoughts, emotions, imagination, and words on what gives you the most exalted state of consciousness and the most happiness and peace of mind. This is what living our bliss means — we follow where our bliss is leading us. By noticing that we have moments of sweetness, peace of mind, and feelings of real love, we can move in the right directions, for these are signposts that say: "This is it, this is a taste and glimpse of what is waiting for you to savor." Turn away from those activities that produce stress, dissatisfaction, and anxiety, for these are the destroyers of life.

This new world does not come about on its own, without our doing our part and acting as if we are already in this new world by turning our attention and cocreative powers in the direction of our new life. Start living now in a way that nurtures you and supports the expression of your talents and heartfelt mission. One small step leads to the next. If you hate your job, do what gives you pleasure and suits your nature, and not what others have told you to do. Don't do what you think will make a lot of money for you but which does not make you happy. What's the point, if you are seeking happiness? You are a real human being, not a computerized machine or a puppet dancing to someone else's tune. All will work out, and when you turn away from the false and focus on the true, you will always have what you need, without stress, fear, or lack.

Seven Ways to Develop Spiritual Consciousness

We are in the process of a major upward shift and great leap forward in the consciousness of humanity. Usually at such times there is first a breakdown and then a breakthrough to the new and improved. *Ascension* means to rise above our current state of awareness into what some call the fourth dimension, and some the fifth — the realm of unconditional love and good fortune for all. When this happens there will be an automatic upgrading of every aspect of life on earth, and anything that does not match this new level of consciousness will disappear for us and continue to exist where it was in the lower, three-dimensional vibration. How do we prepare to take full advantage of this infrequent and most auspicious opportunity that is coming? "Act as if you are as you desire to be, and you will be" is a popular metaphysical principle which teaches us that, whatever we desire to attain, we must have the consciousness that corresponds to it, that has the same vibration.

When unconditional love is our state of mind and emotion, then naturally, by the principle of magnetism, we will draw to us people and situations that correspond perfectly with our consciousness, and the people and situations that do not match will be repelled. Water seeking its own level demonstrates how this works. We can witness this principle at work in business. The person who gets the job must be able to perform the work with proficiency. His consciousness, including his knowledge, experience, and attitude, qualifies him — his vibration matches the vibration required for the work. In this same way, we become qualified to attain whatever we desire, spiritually or materially. Like attracts like. The following are some suggestions for how to re-create yourself and your life around your spiritual nature and give yourself the benefits of a Spirit-centered life.

1. Listen to the most inspiring and heavenly words and sound vibrations possible and avoid the low-level ones.

2. Speak, chant, and sing the words and sounds that make you feel peaceful, inspired, and as blissful as possible. These transcendental sound vibrations will purify your consciousness and the space where you are, and raise the consciousness of all souls on the earth.

3. Keep your mind situated in the transcendental spiritual realm all the time by remembering God and perceiving life through spiritual eyes.

4. Perceive each person and living entity as a soul, and treat each with kindness.

5. Pray to God for guidance and assistance and maintain an attitude of gratitude to God.

6. Do your work with love and enthusiasm as an offering to God for the happiness, good health, and welfare of others.

7. Perceive the Great Spirit as the Creator behind creation, and know it is all a manifestation of God's love for us.

Uni-verse

The universe is one song, one verse, one holographic, harmonic resonance and projection from the superior, spiritual realm, which is the prototype for all that exists in the universe. The Bible tells us: "In the beginning was the Word, and the Word was with God, and the Word was God" (John 1:1). This teaches us that a specific transcendental sound vibration, first as the thought and then the desire to create, followed by the spoken word of the Creator, manifested the entire universe and all that is in it. Science validates the idea that all things have a frequency signature. According to Vedic wisdom, this first sound vibration from the mouth of God was *Aum*. Aum is one of the holy names of God. God created the universe from the potency of his own holy name that contains the female and male aspects of God, including us.

Because the universe and all that is in it was created by sound, sound pervades everything in one magnificent, cosmic symphony. "As above, so below" teaches us that we can know about the spiritual world by noticing what appears in the material world. The music of the spheres in the material universe tells us that the spiritual world is also pervaded by a transcendental symphony, the song of God and Goddess making love to one another. To hear this purely spiritual music, we must listen with our spiritual ears, which develop as we acquire a taste for the sublime and sweet.

Celestial Singers

Singing angels are called Gandharvas in Eastern teachings. Angels exist in most religions and are considered messengers from the spiritual world who help us in times of need. Once when I was on the edge of leaving my body, an invisible but audible choir of angelic beings sang the Aum sound to me for three days, until I was strong enough to leave Kathmandu, Nepal, and return to the United States. Their continual singing of the holy name of God healed my body. Because words unite us with the objects that those words describe, the holy names of God manifest God-consciousness. When we have God-consciousness, we have everything, and all possibilities are then available to us.

Creation is the product of God the Father dancing eternally with his lady, the Supreme Goddess, our Divine Mother, to the intricate steps of the music of her laws, called nature. Their sensual dance of supreme pleasure produces the infinite variety of manifested forms in nature throughout all universes, dimensions, and realms. The One God with two parts, male and female, which are inconceivably, simultaneously, one and different, is always engaged in loving pastimes of divine pleasures and sensual union.

Sound Vibration

All things are manifested from sound and feeling vibrations, because souls are feeling bodies. Just as the universe is a musical instrument, so are our bodies. The head is made partly of bones, which are crystals of communication. Within the skull are resonator chambers called sinuses. When used properly by a singer who combines breath placement, mental focus, and projection, the results are beautiful sounds that thrill both the singer and the listener. Through the same process, chanters and meditators gain entrance into the spiritual realms and higher dimensions. Torsion physics explains how consciousness creates and affects the cosmos and the human condition.

The mind and emotions are the repositories of all human magnetism. Vibrations of thoughts and emotions pervade every atom of the body and act as magnets drawing to us their equivalents in people, things, physical conditions, and circumstances. Thoughts and words move from consciousness and through the various dimensions of material energy by first taking form as geometric shapes, invisible to the human eye, called sacred geometry. These various geometric shapes are the basic building blocks of physical forms. Consciousness is transformed into matter in this way.

Some researchers claim the Great Pyramid in Egypt was built to resemble the abilities of the human body, including the brain and glands, and that it was designed to function as an interdimensional communication and travel device to be used for intergalactic travel by means of thought vibrations and intention. The body temple is also a *merkabah* (vehicle or chariot) that takes the soul to the portal of the spiritual world at the moment of death, leaving behind the old, material body, when the holy spiritual body has become fully activated through unconditional love of God.

The human brain contains the pineal gland, also called the third eye, which gives us entrance into the inner planes of reality and serves as a receiver for revelations and images from the higher dimensions. David Wilcock, a consciousness researcher and hyperdimensional scientist, has found that the pineal gland can be used for intergalactic and out-of-body travel, as well as for ascension. It is interesting to note that the pineal gland contains water, rods, and cones, as our regular eyes do, but that the third eye is activated when the regular eyes are closed. From this, I gather that the pineal gland is perhaps a mirror that reflects the spiritual universe and higher dimensions to what we call our imagination and dreams. We may think that our dreams are not real, but they are real at a frequency different from that of the material, three-dimensional reality. Higher dimensions are not perceivable by our physical eyes, but they are by our third eye.

Healing sounds bring the mind and body into balance. A healthy body has a frequency different from that of a diseased body, and when we use healing frequencies the cells and energies within the body realign with health. Some people use a Rife machine for this purpose in healing. Our bodies are composed of vibrations, so naturally they respond to vibrations positive and negative. We can sense the vibrations that people and locations send out. It's a good idea to avoid anyone or any place that doesn't feel good to us, and to keep company with people around whom we feel good. Businesses that are set up in locations where other businesses have failed, or where the location does not have a good feeling, will almost always fail because something energetically is happening at that specific location.

Emotions and Sounds Affect Water

Dr. Masaru Emoto's photos of water crystals clearly show how loving and happy thoughts, feelings, and words affect water crystals in a beautiful way. Sad and mad thoughts turn water crystals into ugly and distorted monster forms. Our bodies are between 60 and 70 percent water, and our lungs perhaps 90 percent. Imagine how our thoughts and feelings are affecting our bodies and all the water on the planet. This seems to suggest that any negative thoughts and depressing thoughts someone has will also affect the water in the bodies of others near them. If we think happy thoughts and thank God for the water while we are drinking it, the water will bless our bodies and heal them. Water then becomes holy water, healing waters. "Living waters" is the name given to spiritual, eternal truths.

Sacred and feel-good music is inspiring to the soul. Violent and sorrowful words and aggressive and harsh sounds activate violence and suffering in our minds and emotions. Loud sounds such as automobile alarms shock the nervous system. This is the power of vibration. Listening to mundane songs of pain, struggle, lost love, and heartache guarantee that we will experience these same emotions and traumatic experiences because we are accepting those words in our subconscious. A singer's sad emotional state can bring us down to that level as we remember and lament what we call losses. Singers are some of the highest paid professionals in the world because of how their songs influence the listener. Songs of sweetness, love, and beauty lift the soul and reflect the music of the spheres, thus drawing sweetness to us. In the culture of India, there are tales of the ecstatically blissful and alluring sounds of Krishna's flute music that captivated the hearts of the Gopis, his most beloved friends. Steven Rosen described the various forms of adulation in his book, *Essential Hinduism*:

> King David preached, "From the rising of the sun to its setting, the name of the Lord is to be praised." (Psalms 113.3); Saint Paul said, "Everyone who calls upon the name of the Lord will be saved." (Romans 10.13); Mohammed, in the Koran (87.2), counseled, "Glorify the name of your Lord, the most high;" Buddha declared, "All who sincerely call upon my name will come to me after death, and I will take them to paradise." (Vows of Amida Buddha, 18); and the Vaishnava scriptures repeatedly assert: "Chant the holy name, chant the holy name, chant the holy name of the Lord...." (*Brihad-Naradiya Purana* 3.8.126).

The Holy Names

Singing songs of love, adoration, and glorification to God makes us feel good because they elevate our consciousness to levels of joy above the dense vibrations of earthly woes. All holy names of God are inspiring, and some names are more inspiring and powerful than others. Mantras are sacred sound vibrations that harmonize our mental and physical vibrations with the Holy Spirit. Mental and emotional balance is the key to creating harmony in our lives and on the earth, and to elevating ourselves to the realm of divine pleasure.

In a golden age, there are no devastating earth changes, for everyone and everything is in perfect harmonic balance. In the previous golden age, humans were able to communicate telepathically, manifest whatever they desired, levitate, and travel anywhere on the earth or within the galaxy simply by the use of mantras. Kardama Muni, a powerful mystic and saint who lived in India during the previous golden age, manifested a magnificent aerial city complete with homes, gardens, waterfalls, and lakes for him and his wife to enjoy during their lovemaking and life together. Our lack of awareness of these possibilities is a symptom of our being covered by dense material energy, which makes us forget who we are as spiritual beings possessing all godlike qualities and powers.

The holy names of God are perfectly balanced, and they exist at such a high vibrational frequency that they act like medicine that cure all the ills of humanity. Spiritual vibrations rid the mind of all negative fear- and lack-based programming. Holy, transcendental sound vibrations manifest ecstatic levels of bliss and love called *prema*. *Prema* is a Sanskrit word for exalted levels of true love and bliss that are uncommon and rarely experienced while a person is still in a material body. The frequency of these levels is so high that our current bodies, made of dense matter, are not able to experience it, though our spiritual bodies are able to. Spiritual love is ever increasing without limit.

There are many holy names for God and his Goddess, and each brings bliss when sung or chanted with attention and love flowing to one's preferred deity. The word *God* is a job description, just like *human being* is a job description. Each person has a name, and usually many names, not just one. We give names of endearment to our closest friends and family members, and there are nicknames as well. Names of God have meanings that pertain to a particular religion's concept of God, such as Almighty, Great Spirit, Jesus, Lord, Krishna, Shiva, Rama, Christ, Allah, Aum, Govinda, Makunda, and Beloved. The list goes on and on because of all the various ways that people perceive the Supreme Being. There are many names for the Divine Mother as well, including Mother Mary, Radha, Shakti, Sita, Durga, Hare, Devi, and Goddess. Each name indicates a quality, power, activity, or relationship.

All names are correct, for God has not one name only, as this would limit the unlimited in our minds and so limit us. God is not limited by our concepts, nor does anyone or any one group have control of God or the Goddess. The problem with sectarianism is war, as if there were many Gods all in competition with each other. For peace and prosperity to prevail upon the earth, we must understand that we have the same God, that we have the right to worship that One God as each chooses, and that we must celebrate the rights of all to religious freedom. The One God is not jealous, is not angry with us, and is not anyone to fear. It is the little gods, each seeking to be superior to the other gods, who are in competition, envious of the other gods, and mean-spirited, as if this will make them better and thus happier. The Bible tells us: "Which of you by taking thought can add one cubit unto his stature?" (Matthew 6:27). Thoughts cannot make us better or worse, we are what we are and this is absolute and unchanging.

There is only One God, with unlimited spiritual qualities, names, forms, and pastimes. Words are vibrations that manifest objects, so speaking and singing the names of God and the Goddess take us to them. This means that the transcendental vibration of the holy names manifests the spiritual vibration of the Divinity where we are and purifies our consciousness and elevates us to the spiritual domain of ever-increasing levels of bliss, love, opulence, powers, and peace, the peace that passes all understanding. The secret place of the most high is the realm of the Great Soul, from which each of us emanates, that place where we go in our meditation, and from which all answers and realizations arise. We are each individual aspects and emanations of this One Great Soul that is all-knowing, all-powerful, all-loving, all-blissful, and everywhere. Whatever is known anywhere is known by the One God and also known by us when we ask for whatever we want to know to be revealed to us. In this way we can understand that we have the same Soul as our Source, so we are one and also different, since each of us is also an individual. *Achintya bheda bheda tattva* means that we are inconceivably, simultaneously, one with and different from God and each other, but never separate, except in a mind that conceives of itself as separate and alone.

Mantras, Chants, and Affirmations

Any mantra you choose will manifest the meaning of the name, because the sound vibration for each mantra has the vibrational power to transfer that vibration to you and your environment. Transcendental sound vibrations are more powerful than any material world vibration, even the most dense and harsh. In the same way that singing a happy song can influence us to feel good, imagine the power of holy, spiritual vibrations and what these can do for us.

We can choose the mantras, chants, songs, and affirmations that we like best. The mantra that I have found gives me the full gamut of spiritual and material benefits, including bliss, peace of mind, and prosperity, is "Hare Krishna Hare Krishna Krishna Krishna Hare Hare, Hare Rama Hare Rama Rama Rama Hare Hare." *Hare* is a name of the Divine Mother, *Krishna* is a name of the Divine Father, meaning all-attractive, and *Rama* is another name of the male God, meaning supreme pleasure. It is suggested that we chant or sing any mantra we choose at least 108 times a day, preferably as many as you can. The more times the better, because with it we are controlling the mind and purifying our consciousness so that we realize our real spiritual and blissful identity.

Aum chanted 24 times, 3 times a day, for at least twenty-one days will have a profound, positive effect on the chanter. With any mantra, focusing on the sound is important. Chanting or singing with your eyes closed while concentrating on the holy sounds can help to activate the pineal gland and give you images of the higher dimensions, as well as answers, solutions, and inspiration.

"Hail Mary full of grace, blessed art thou among women and blessed is the fruit of thy womb, Jesus" is a classic Catholic chant. "I love you, God" and "I love you, Goddess" are both excellent mantras that still the mind and help us to feel and flow the river of love. Do your research and choose the holy names and mantras that best suit you and what you want to attain. "Aum Laxmi Narayan swaha" is an excellent prosperity mantra, for when you chant it you are using the temple of your body to speak the holy names of the Goddess of Fortune, Laxmi, and her husband, Lord Narayan, who gives wealth and opulence. "Aum Shanti" is a prayer for peace of mind. When you repeat the mantras and prayers of your choice, allow their sounds and meanings to sink deep into your subconscious and heart, and accept them so the power of the mantras can manifest for you.

Welcome to the Spiritual World

There is no new world to be ushered in, for God's kingdom is already here. . . . Rather the kingdom is inside you.

JESUS, IN THE GOSPEL OF THOMAS

I have presented my case for bliss, and for how to attain it now and forever because you are eternity itself. This leads me to summarize what I have written for your pleasure. No all-satisfying permanent happiness can be found in material objects, which is why material scientists have failed to make humanity contented, happy, or even healthy. Where is this happiness to be found? The answer is: within ourselves. It cannot be found in anything or anyone outside of our Self and ourselves in relationship with our Soul, the Soul of every soul.

This continual stream of happiness is flowing at all times from our Heart of Hearts all through our bodies, but we cannot perceive or experience this bliss as long as we believe that we do not have it. The belief that we are not happy is what makes us unhappy. Unhappiness is the cause of all personal and global problems, for it is only unhappy people trying to get happiness who commit violence on others or themselves.

Because God is the totality of the all and everything, then it just makes sense to understand that if we want bliss, opulence, prosperity, and love we must seek it from the reservoir of all this and more. God is with us, always giving us the kingdom, just as a loving parent offers all she has to her children; however, the children must be willing to receive all that is being given. Just as we cannot get honey from a rock but only from a source of honey, we can only get the love and wealth we are seeking from the source of love and wealth that is the Soul of every soul. Turn within and greet your eternal Beloved and get back into communication, in case you have forgotten. Once we recognize this same Soul as also present with every other living entity and everywhere present as well, then we are truly always in the spiritual world, for Spirit is all there is and we are never alone. Then we can find pleasure in everything and everywhere, for we take our pleasure with us and we allow the river of bliss and love to continuously express through us as us. Love is not something that happens to us — it is what we are made of — so what could be more painful than not being ourselves? There is no greater pleasure than being your true self all the time regardless of what others say or do or anything happening in the outer world of change. Live in a constant state of appreciation and gratitude to your God. Remember God and never forget God, and surrender into the loving arms of your eternal Father and Mother, whose favorite child you are. Let your light shine brightly and give the glory to God, and then you become that channel and vehicle of Divine bliss, intelligence, creativity, and opulence expressing wherever you are.

Remember

The Great Spirit within, which is everywhere present and all-knowing, gives us truth, just as the Great Spirit gave it to great souls before us. We get truth when we sincerely ask for it. Truth is eternal and inexhaustible. We receive a revelation when we are most ready for it. The souls of the great spiritual thinkers of yesteryear, who now live spiritually, are still teaching and helping us, just as they did when they were in this world. When we are attracted to Jesus, Mother Mary, Caitanya, a specific angel, or some other higher being of pure love, or we go directly to God Within and request assistance, we are given help.

Divine revelation is absolute truth, but the receiver's prejudices, motives, and cultural and religious training often flavor it. For this reason we must trust our conscience to be the final judge, the ultimate discriminator. When we study the lives of great souls, or learn of the amazing activities of the demigods and goddesses and other beings who reside in the spiritual universe, we learn what is possible for us. These higher beings are working for and with us as we awaken by remembering who we are.

Our work is not simply for us to be receptacles of sacred knowledge. We, too, are meant to knock at the gate of the treasure house of the boundless reservoir of truth from which the former mystics and brilliant geniuses drew their wealth. We must seek from the source of truth within, the fountainhead of supreme knowledge, where all who ask receive. Dip into the reservoir of soul pleasure through loving reciprocation, and receive all you desire. Anyone can do so. We are meant to do this, we must do this. Live your bliss. Let it flow.

May you continue to be blessed with all manner of ever-increasing good fortune.

With love,
Terry

Acknowledgments

Georgia Hughes, my editor at New World Library, is at the top of my list of acknowledgments for all the work she has done to help me to get my ideas into a presentable form. I must also acknowledge the others at New World Library who worked on this book for their methodical work of making my teaching understandable to the reader, as I am a right-brained person for whom organization of ideas in a logical order is challenging. I thank Ginny Weisman for her efforts in attaining the perfect publisher.

No one does anything alone, and every person in my life has been a gift to me, for which I am grateful. Special mention goes to Ganesha and Saraswati for their continual inspiration and guidance. I acknowledge you, the reader, for it is my desire that something within the pages of this book will become a catalyst for your God-realization and for your life's work to make an enormous, positive, and loving difference in the lives of all who partake of your offerings.

Endnotes

Introduction

Page xiv, *Great spirits have always encountered violent opposition from mediocre minds*: Abraham Pais, *Einstein Lived Here* (New York: Oxford University Press, 1994), p. 219.

Page xiv, *The usual approach of science of constructing a mathematical model*: Stephen Hawking, *A Brief History of Time* (New York: Bantam, 1998), 190.

Chapter 3: Expand beyond Self-Imposed Limitations into the Realms of Greatness

Page 61, *Those who cherish a beautiful vision*: James Allen, *As You Think*, ed. Marc Allen (Novato, CA: New World Library, 1998), 75, 79.

Page 82, *Every heart that has beat strong and cheerfully*: Robert Louis Stevenson, *The Works of Robert Louis Stevenson*, Valima Edition, vol. II (New York: Charles Scribner's Sons, 1922), 130.

Chapter 8: Entrance into the Realm of Divine Pleasures

Page 209, *Steven Rosen described the various forms of adulation*: Steven J. Rosen, *Essential Hinduism* (Westport, CT: Praeger Publishers, 2006), p. 219.

Recommended Reading

Bhaktivedanta, A. C. *Bhagavad-Gita as It Is* (New York: Collier Books, 1972).

———. *Srimad Bhagavatam* (Los Angeles: Bhaktivedanta Book Trust, 1983).

Holmes, Ernest. *Science of Mind* (New York: Dodd Mead, 1938).

Kapoor, O. B. L. *Lord Chaitanya* (Mathura, India: Srila Badri-narayana Bhagavata Bhushana, 1997).

Lad, Vasant. *Ayurveda: The Science of Self-Healing* (Twin Lakes, WI: Lotus Press, 2004).

Lamsa, George M. *Holy Bible: From the Ancient Eastern Text* (San Francisco: HarperSanFrancisco, 1968).

Meyer, Marvin W. *The Gnostic Discoveries* (San Francisco: HarperSanFrancisco, 2005).

———. *The Secret Teachings of Jesus* (New York: Random House, 1984).

Moritz, Andreas. *The Amazing Liver and Gallbladder Flush* (Landrum, SC: Ener-Chi Wellness Press), 2007.

Pagels, Elaine, and Karen L. King. *Reading Judas* (New York: Penguin, 2007).

Robbins, John. *May All Be Fed*: *Diet for a New World* (New York: Avon Books, 1992).

Thakura, Vrndavana Dasa. *Caitanya Bhagavata* (Vrindaban, India: Rasbihari lal & Sons, n.d.).

About the Author

*T*erry Cole-Whittaker is considered by many to be one of the premier motivational and inspirational speakers and teachers in the world. She was the CEO of her own corporation of forty employees, six hundred volunteers, and seven teaching centers throughout California. Her Emmy-winning weekly television ministry program was syndicated in over four hundred markets in the USA, Canada, Mexico, Puerto Rico, and Guam and reached millions. Her five bestselling books highlight the body of her work. *What You Think of Me Is None of My Business*, a classic, pioneering book on personal power and motivation, is still in print after twenty years. Her other books include *How to Have More in a Have-Not World*, *Love and Power in a World Without Limits*, and *Dare to Be Great*. She has appeared on over eight hundred television and radio programs, including *Oprah*, *Larry King Live*, and *Good Morning America*, and has been featured on the front page of the *Wall Street Journal* and in *Time*, *Newsweek*, *Family Circle*, and many other magazines and newspapers. Terry travels extensively giving seminars, retreats, and keynote addresses to both spiritual and entrepreneurial groups. She lives in Los Angeles, California. Her website is www.terrycolewhittaker.com.

NEW WORLD LIBRARY is dedicated to publishing books and other media that inspire and challenge us to improve the quality of our lives and the world.

We are a socially and environmentally aware company, and we strive to embody the ideals presented in our publications. We recognize that we have an ethical responsibility to our customers, our staff members, and our planet.

We serve our customers by creating the finest publications possible on personal growth, creativity, spirituality, wellness, and other areas of emerging importance. We serve New World Library employees with generous benefits, significant profit sharing, and constant encouragement to pursue their most expansive dreams.

As a member of the Green Press Initiative, we print an increasing number of books with soy-based ink on 100 percent postconsumer-waste recycled paper. Also, we power our offices with solar energy and contribute to nonprofit organizations working to make the world a better place for us all.

Our products are available
in bookstores everywhere.
For our catalog, please contact:

New World Library
14 Pamaron Way
Novato, California 94949

Phone: 415-884-2100 or 800-972-6657
Catalog requests: Ext. 50
Orders: Ext. 52
Fax: 415-884-2199
Email: escort@newworldlibrary.com

To subscribe to our electronic newsletter, visit
www.newworldlibrary.com